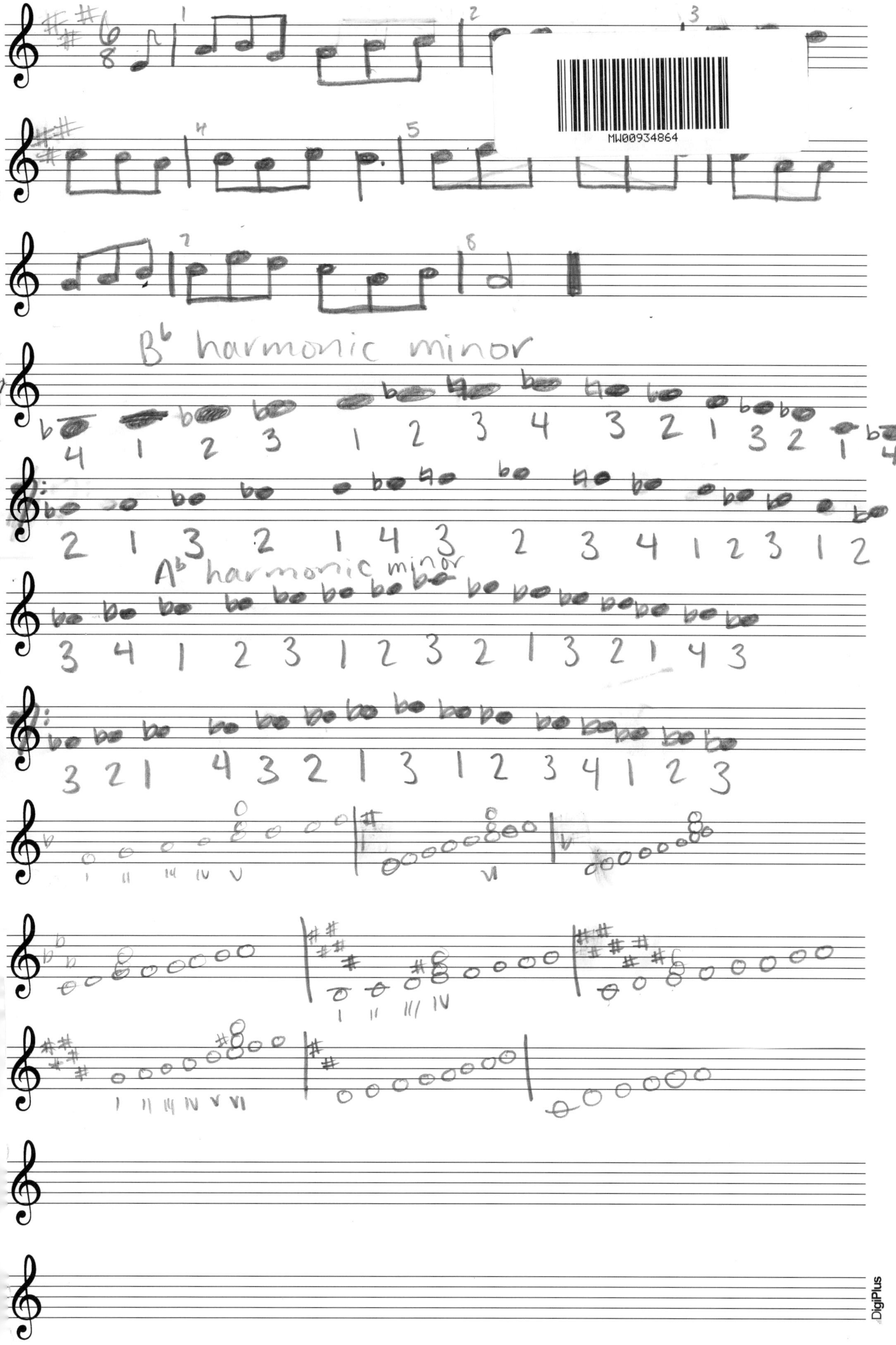
B♭ harmonic minor
A♭ harmonic minor

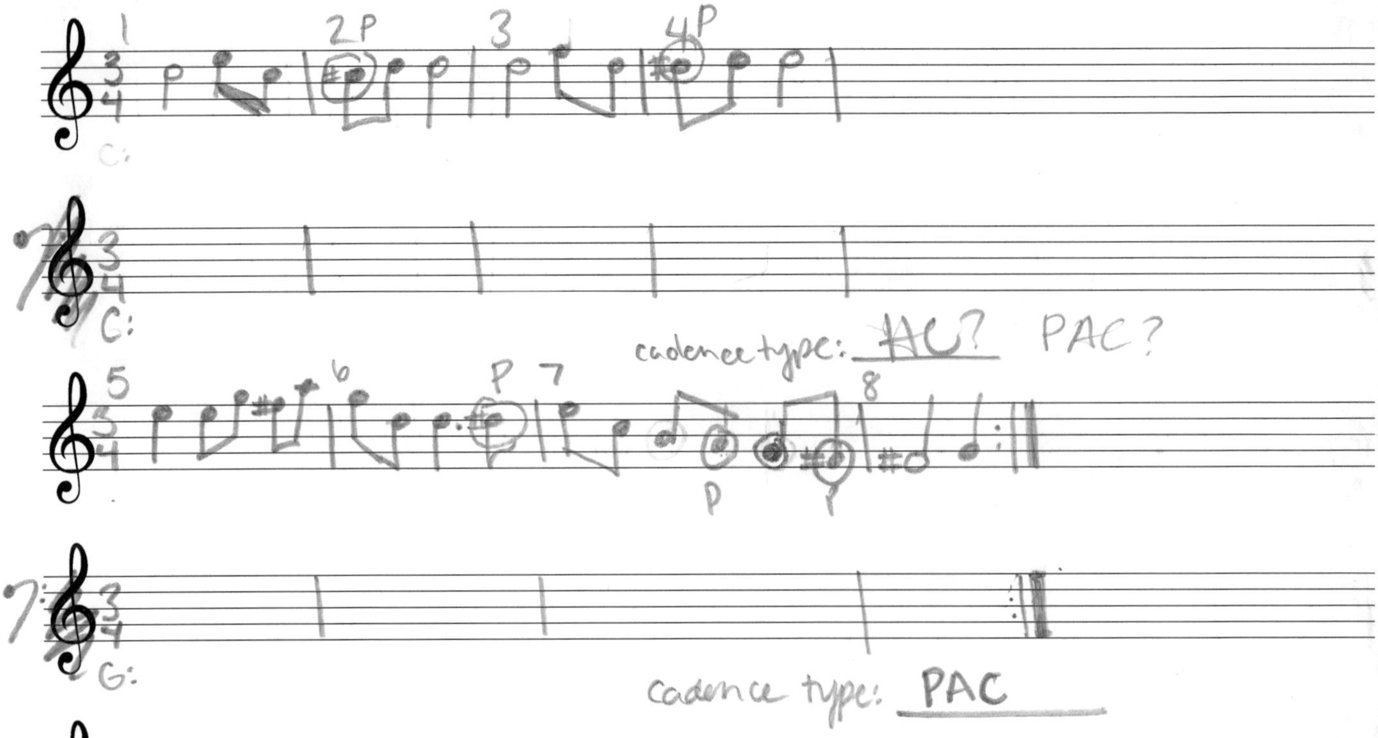
C:
cadence type: HC? PAC?
G:
cadence type: PAC

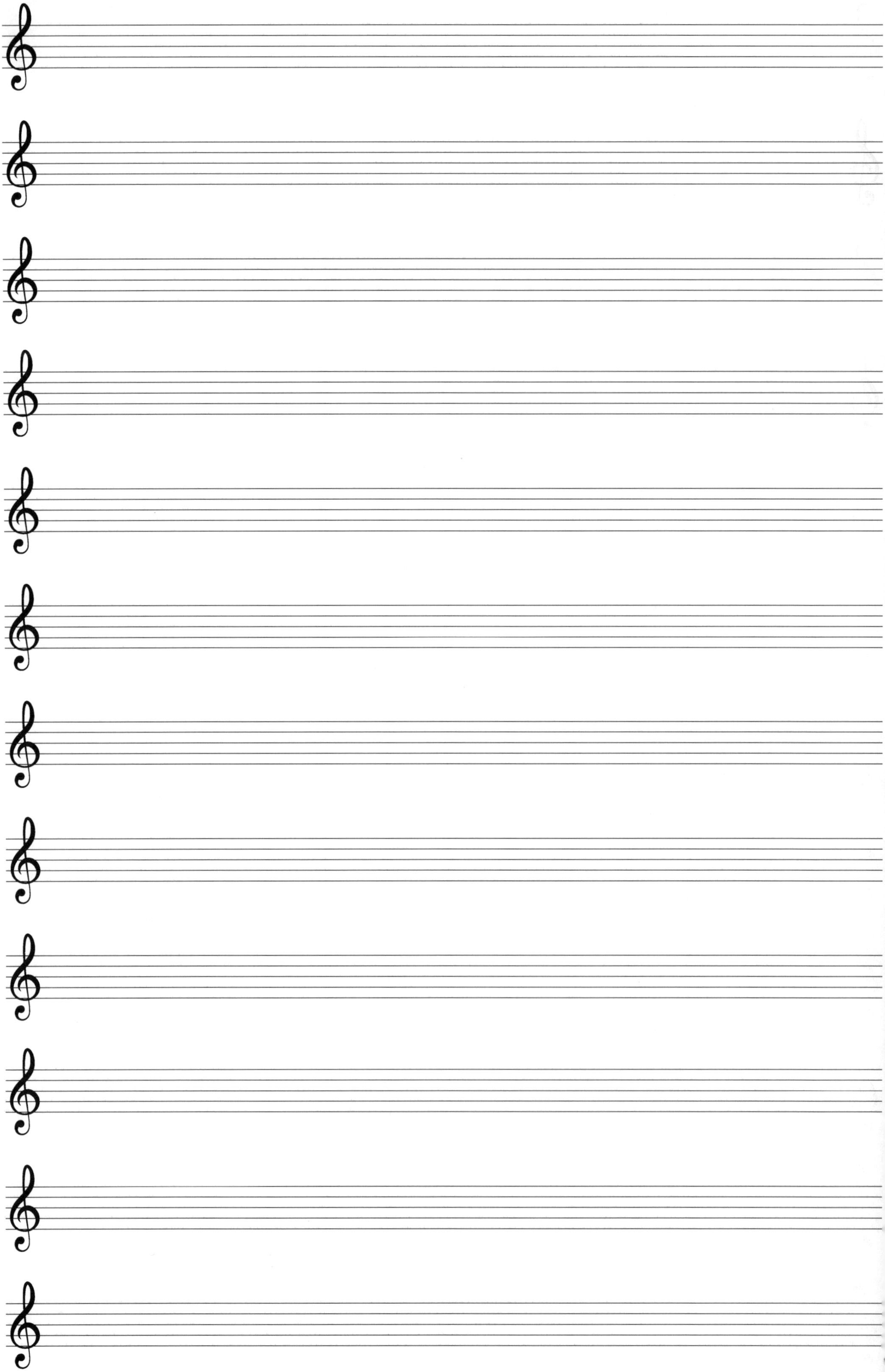

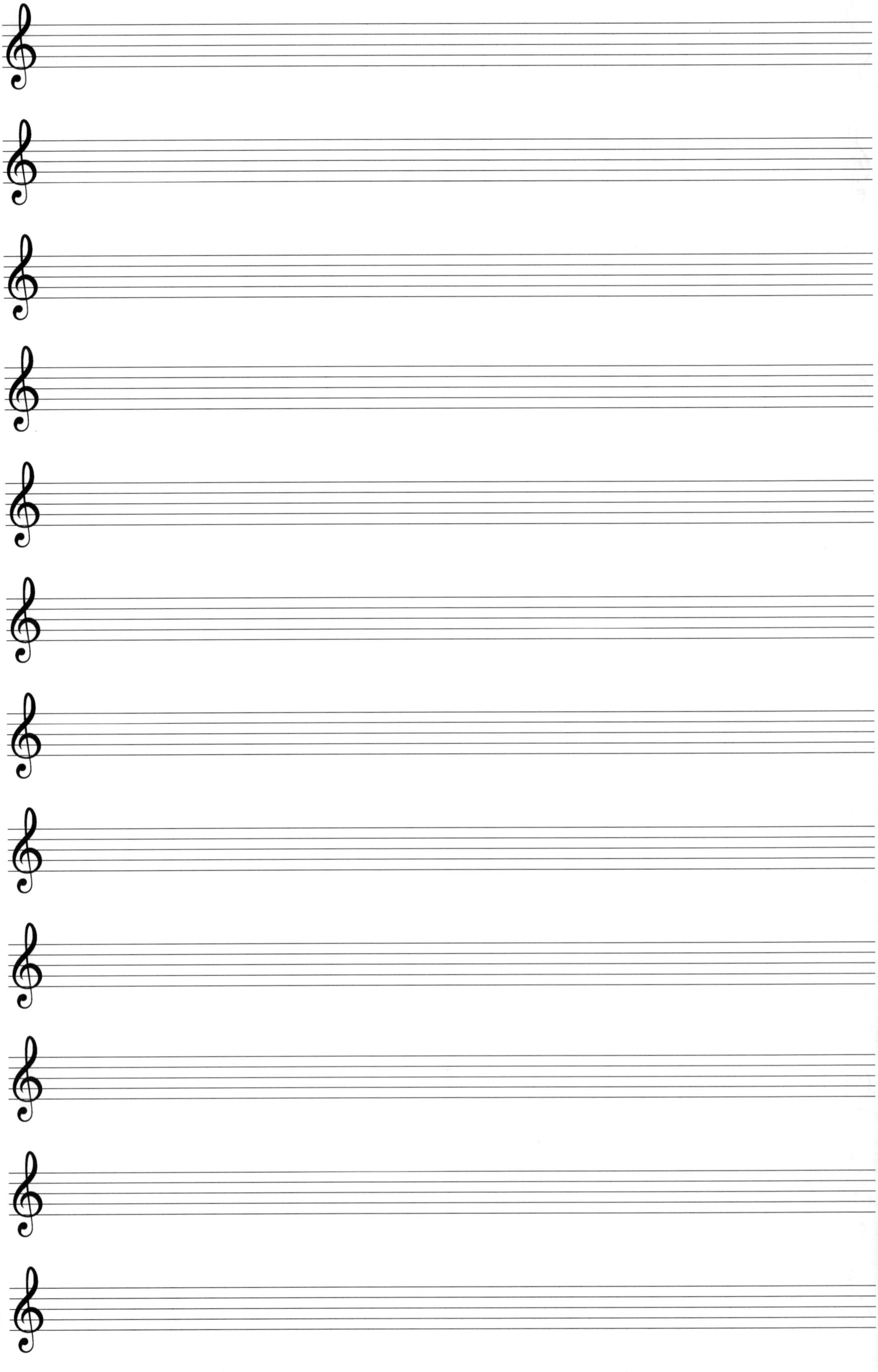

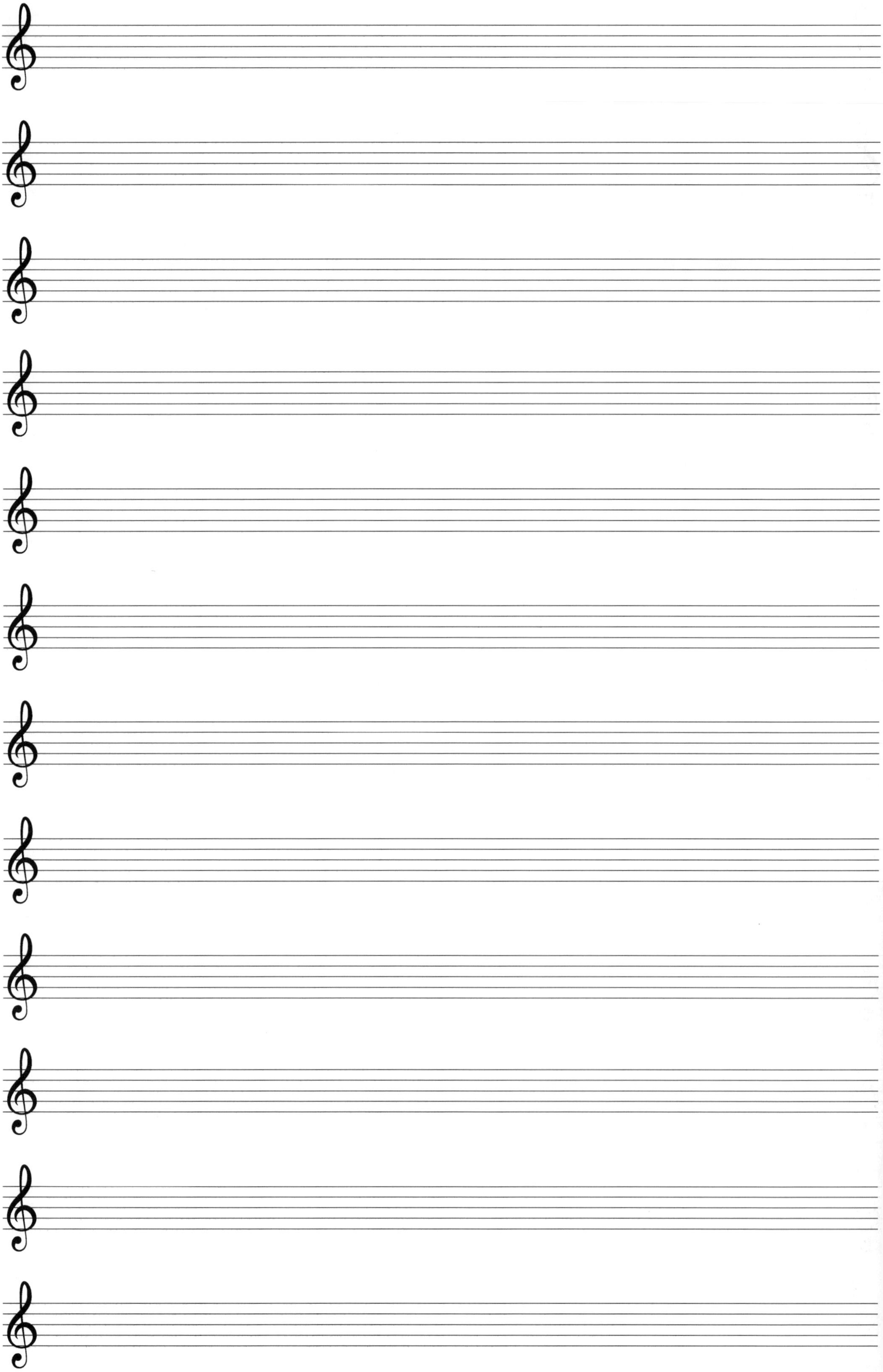

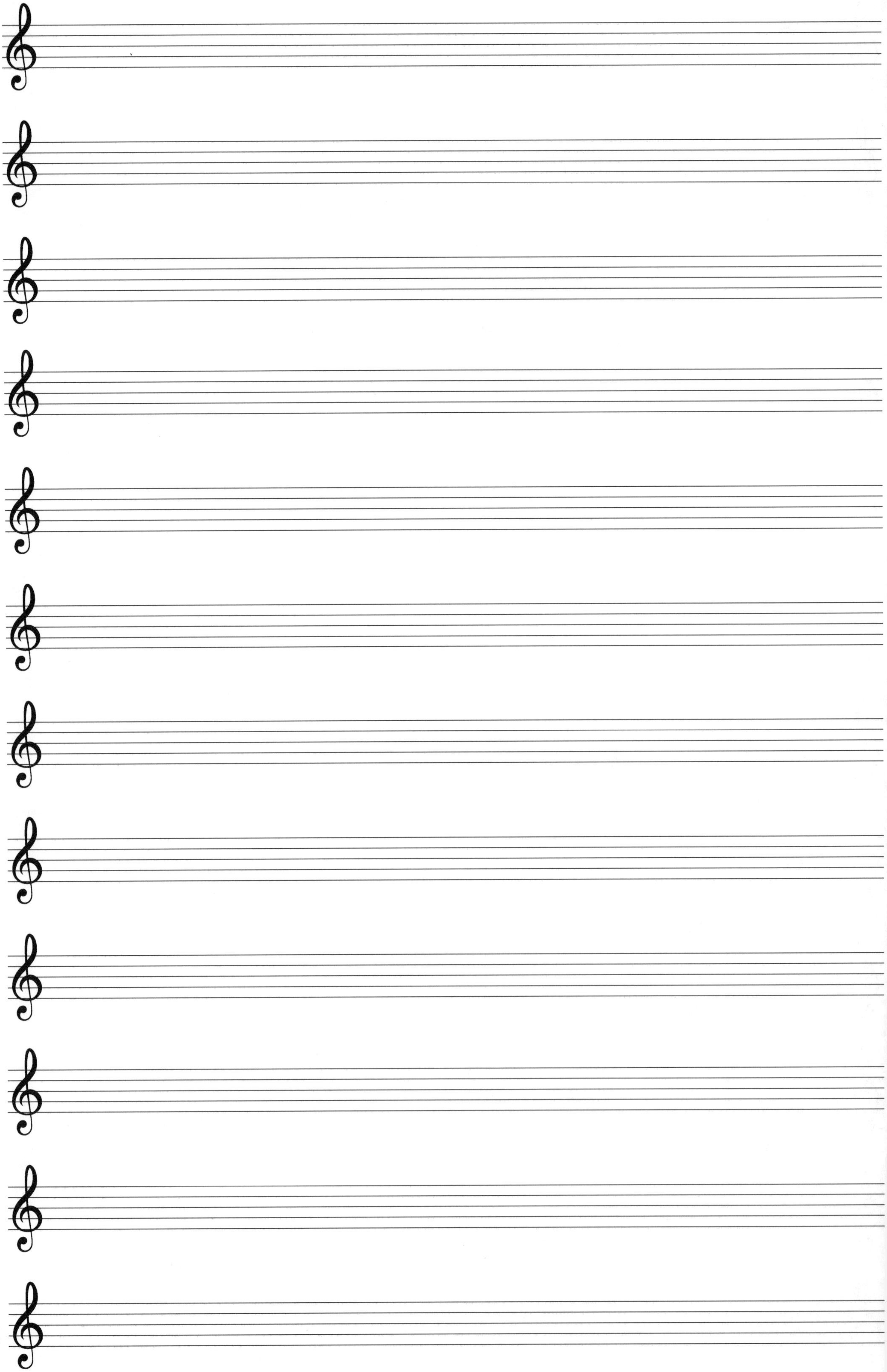

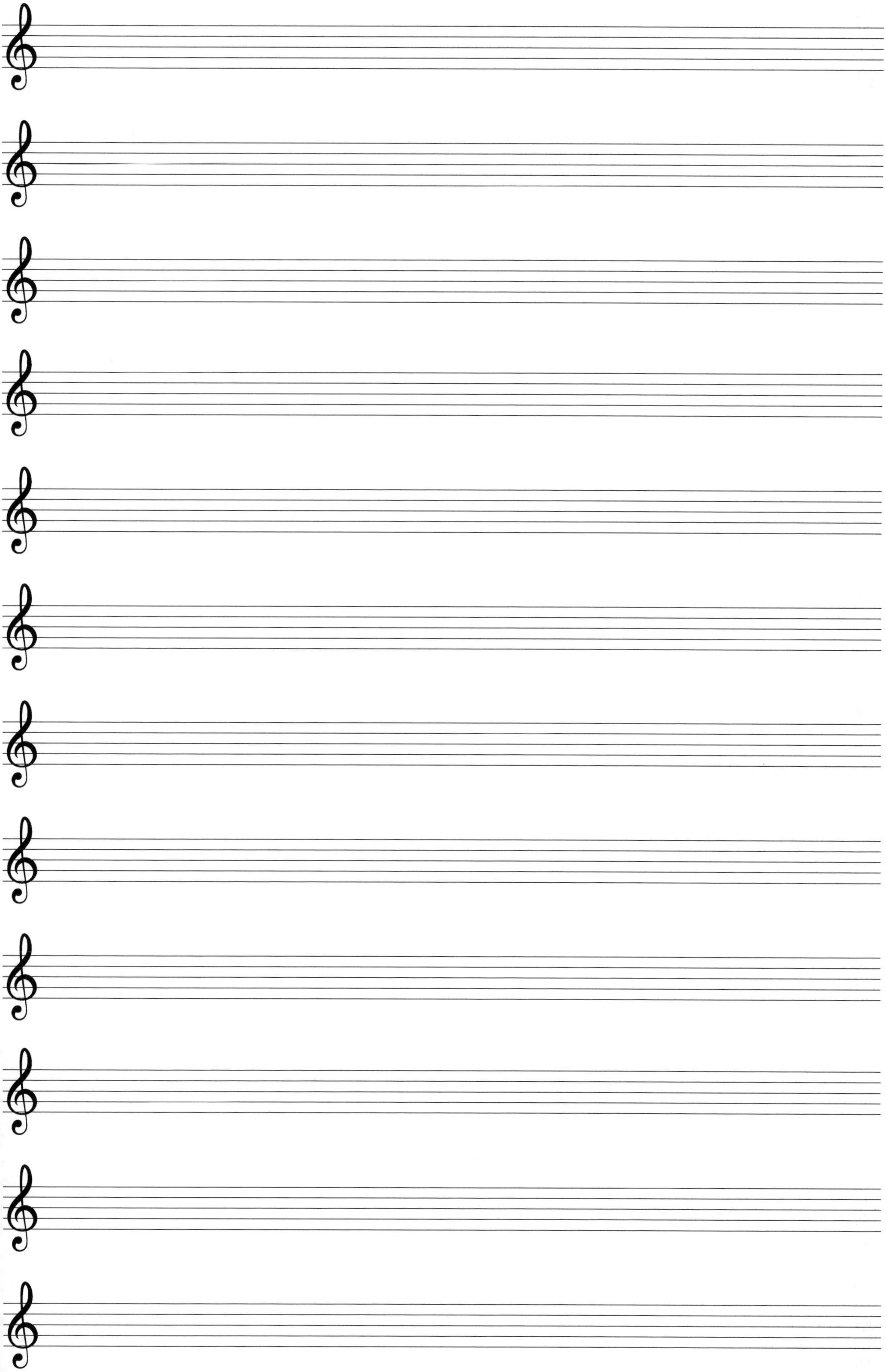

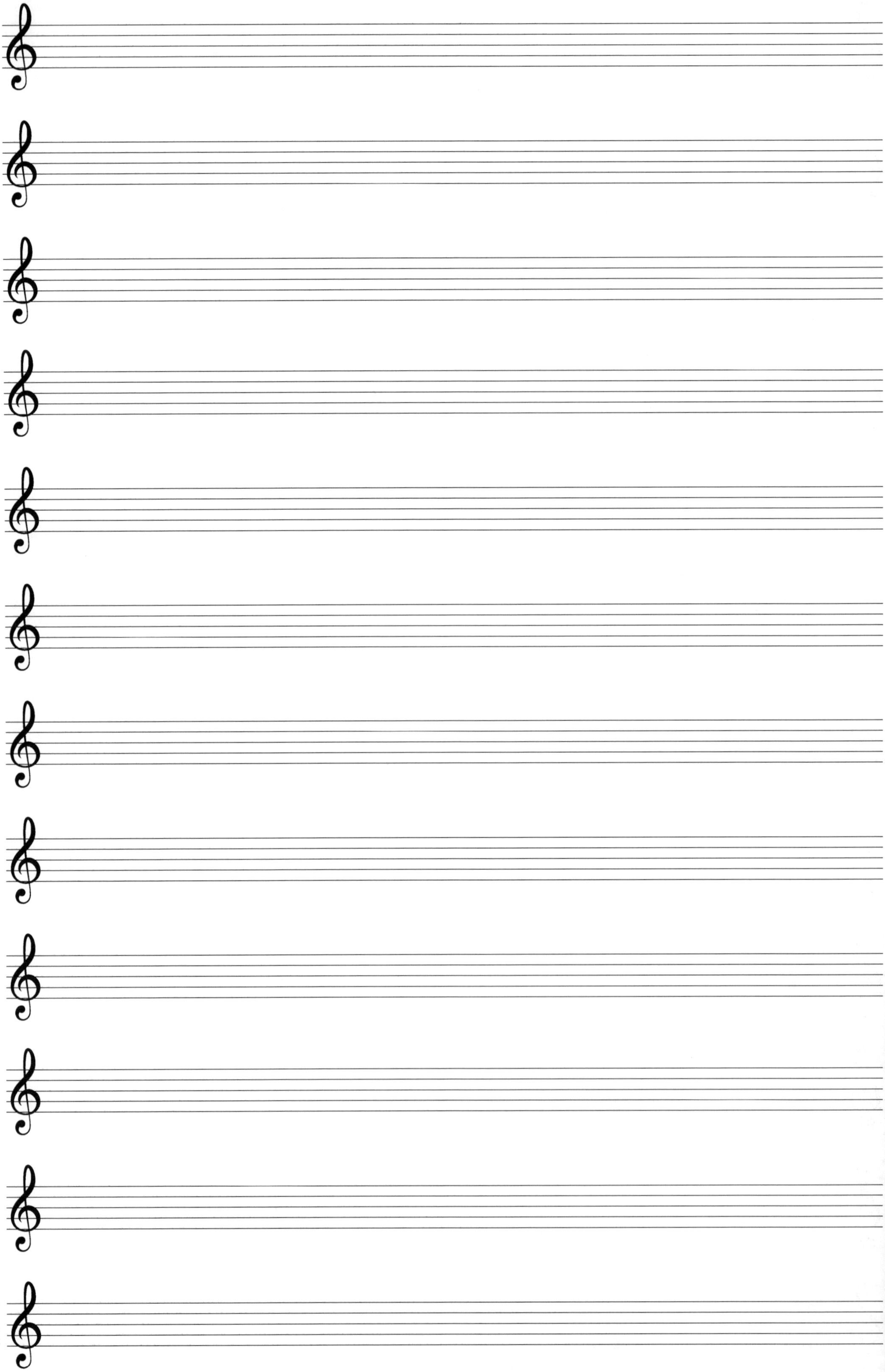

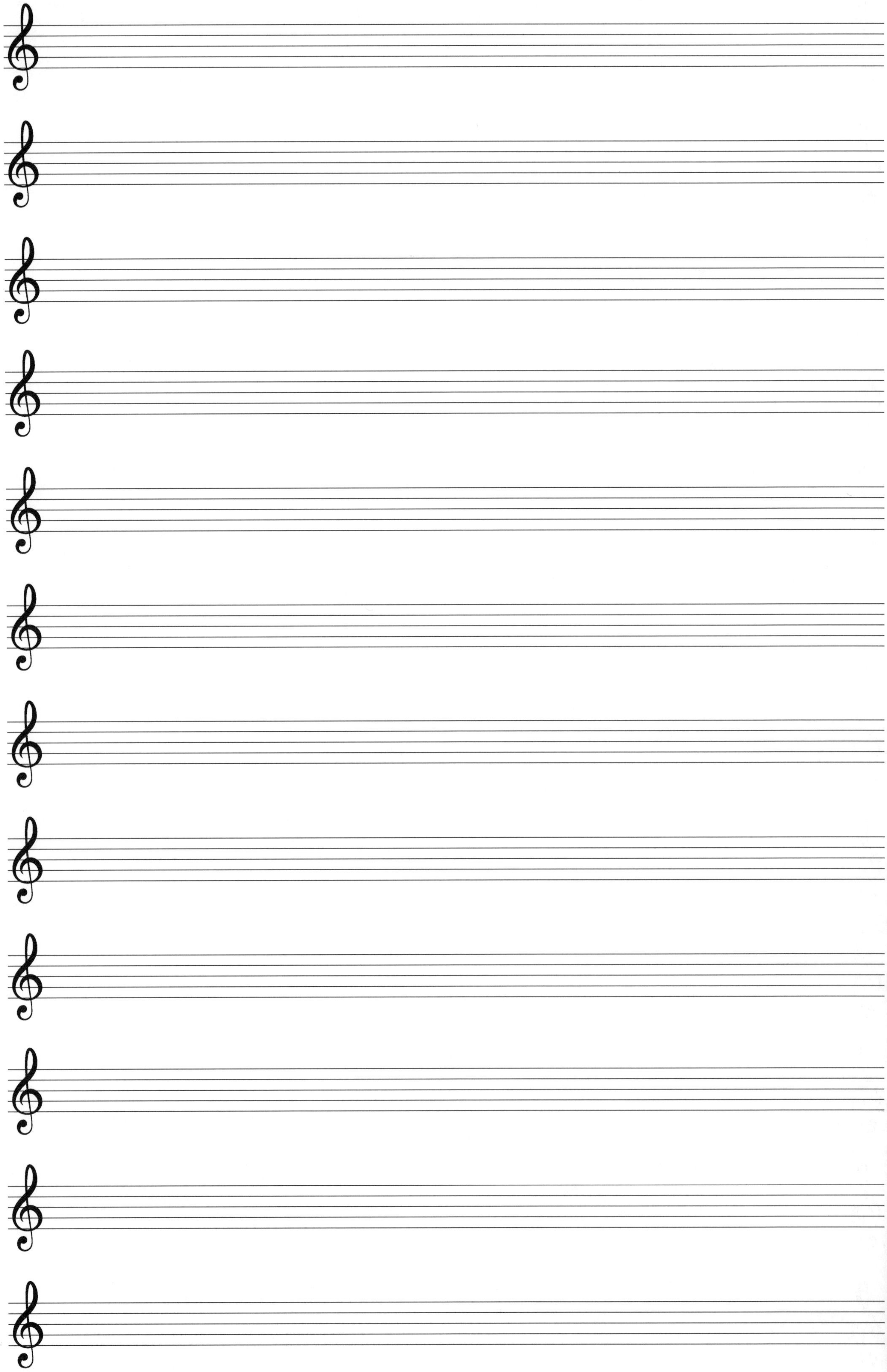

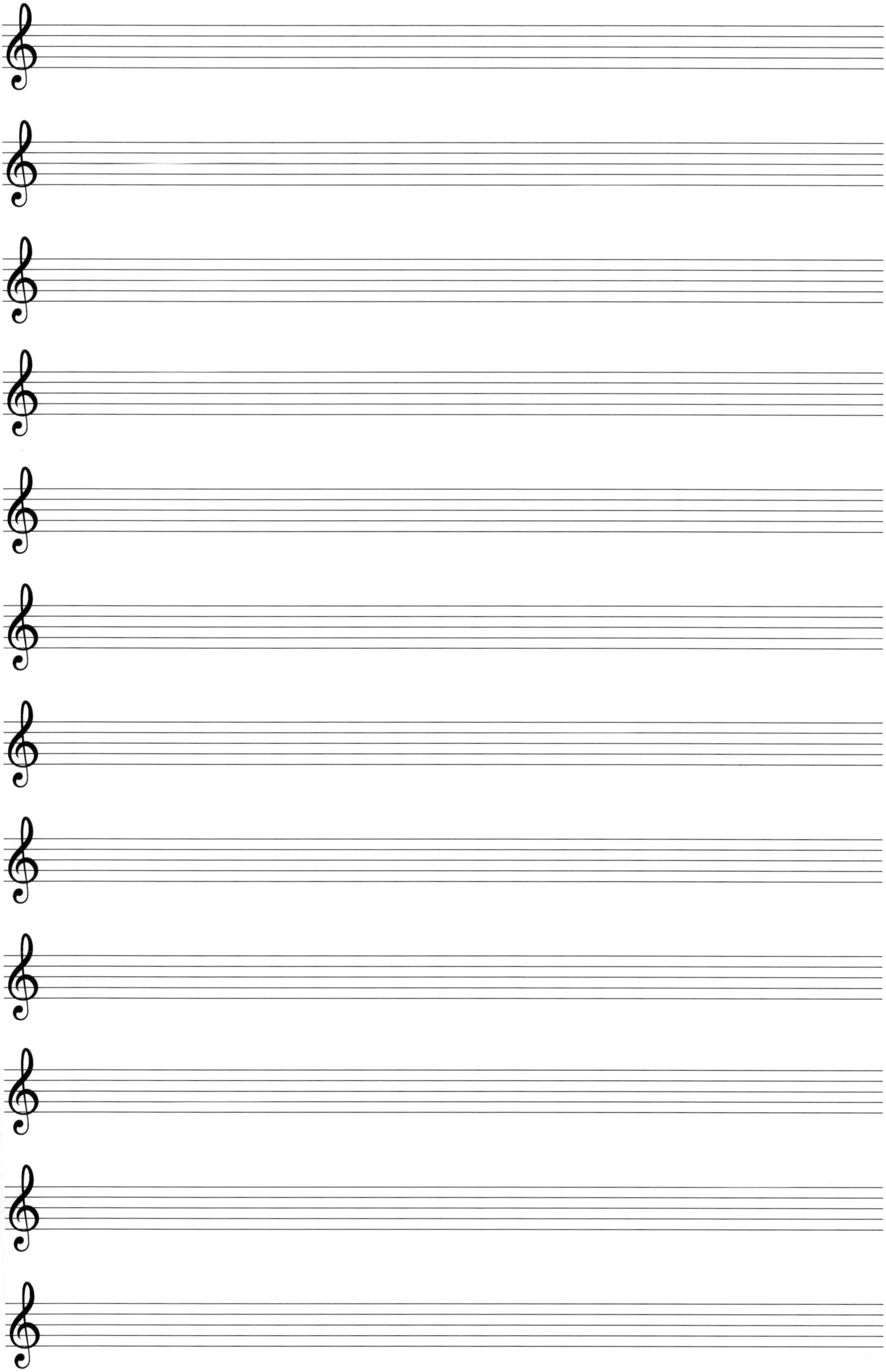

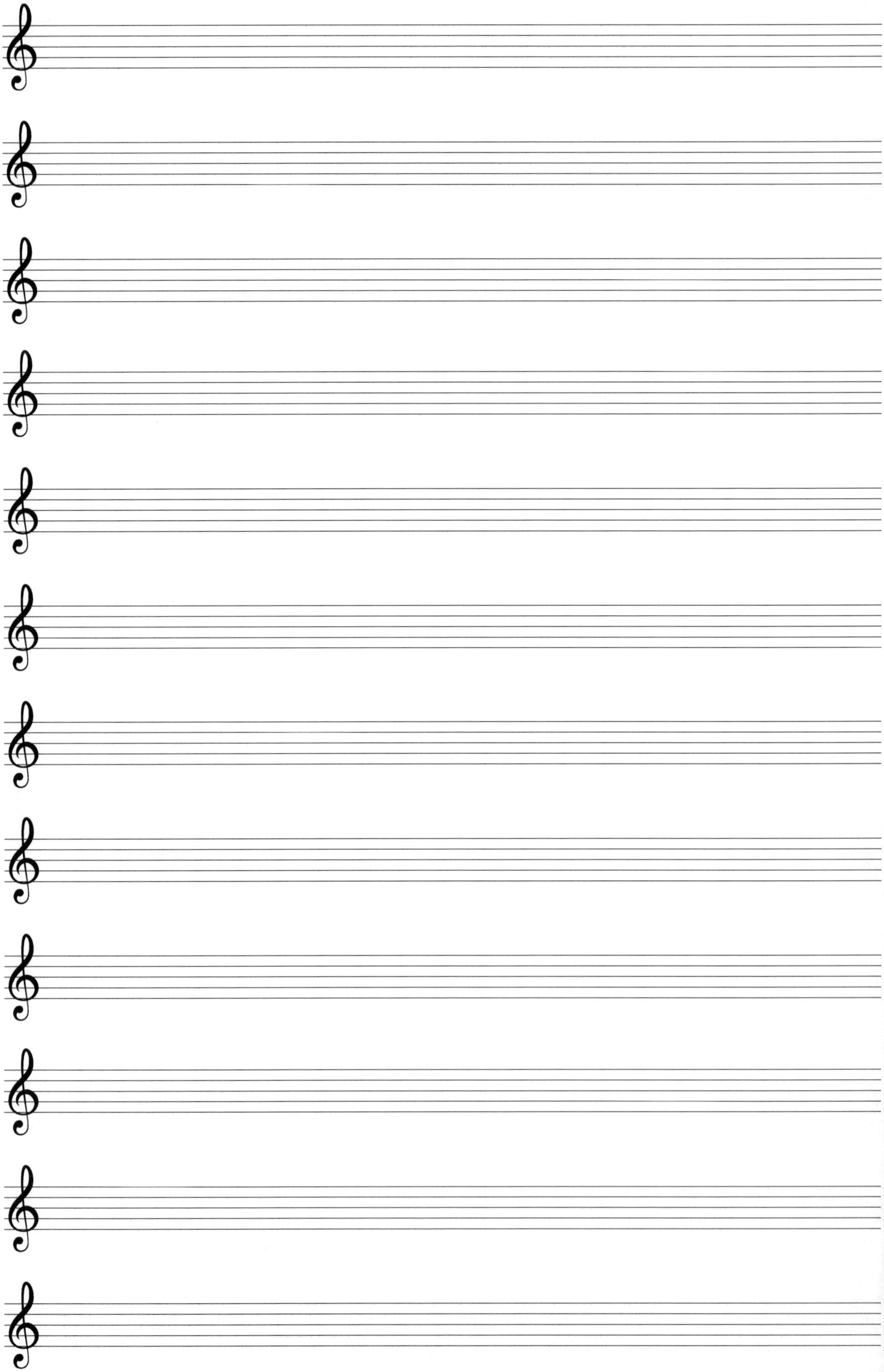

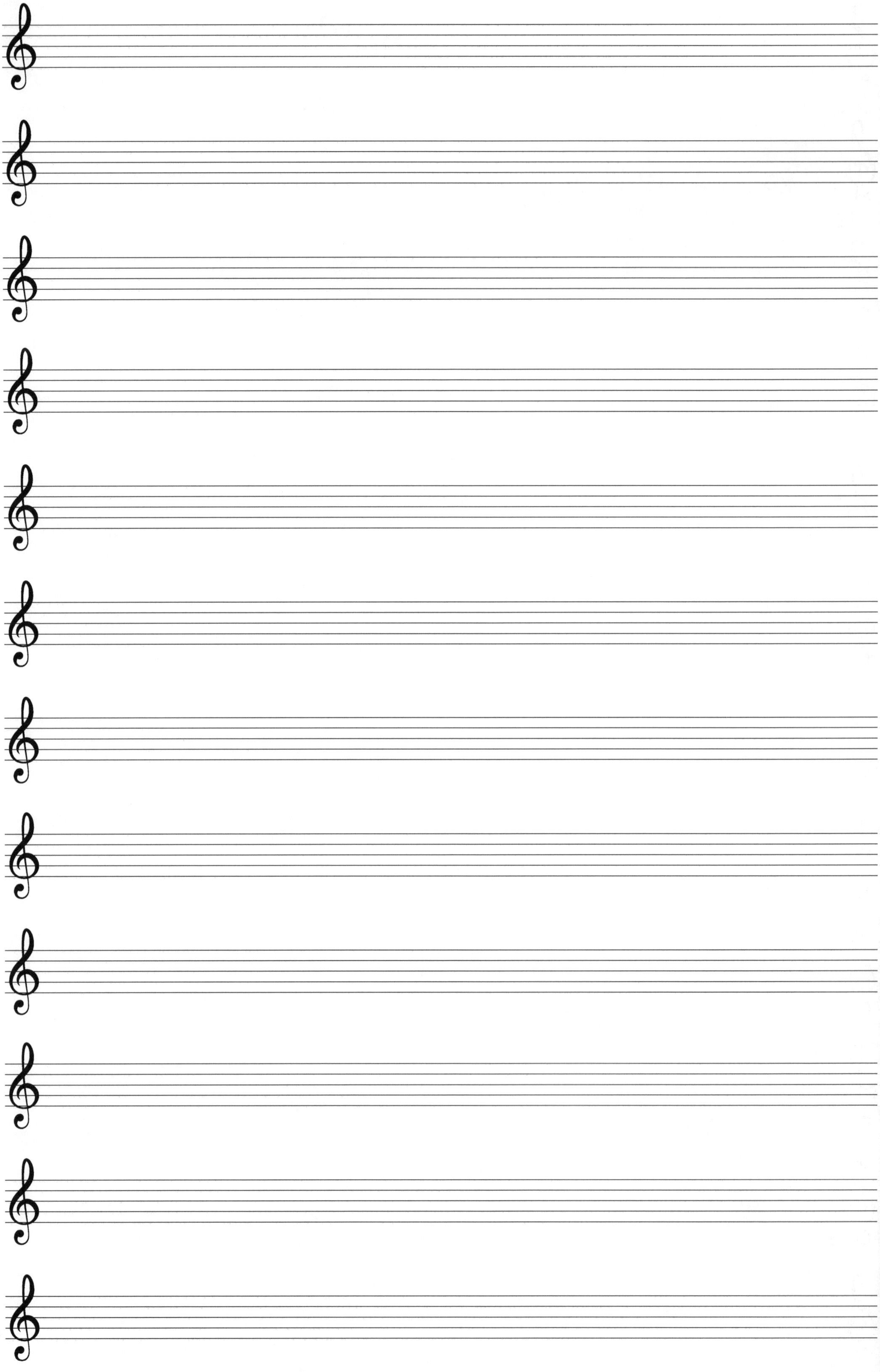

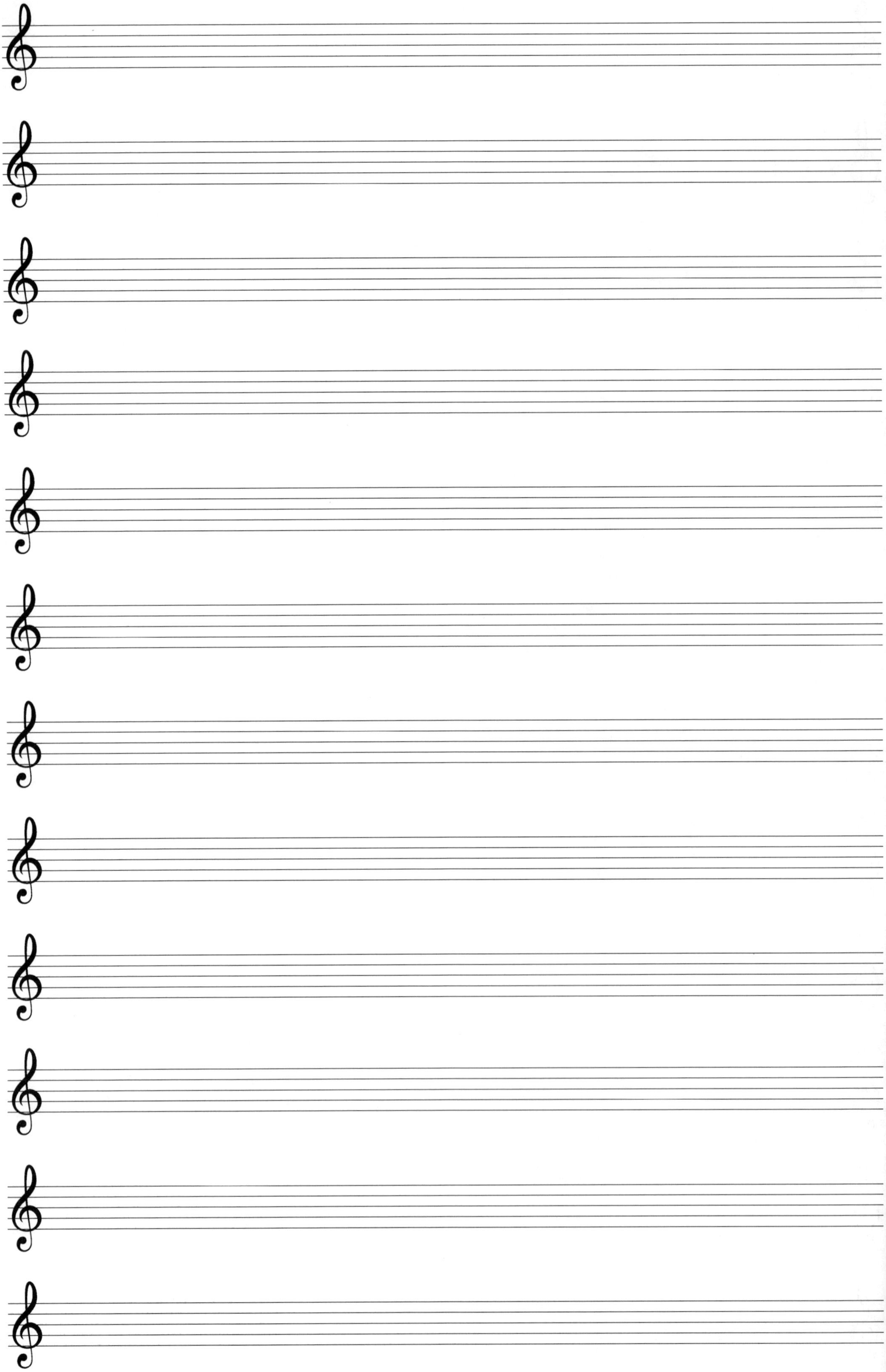

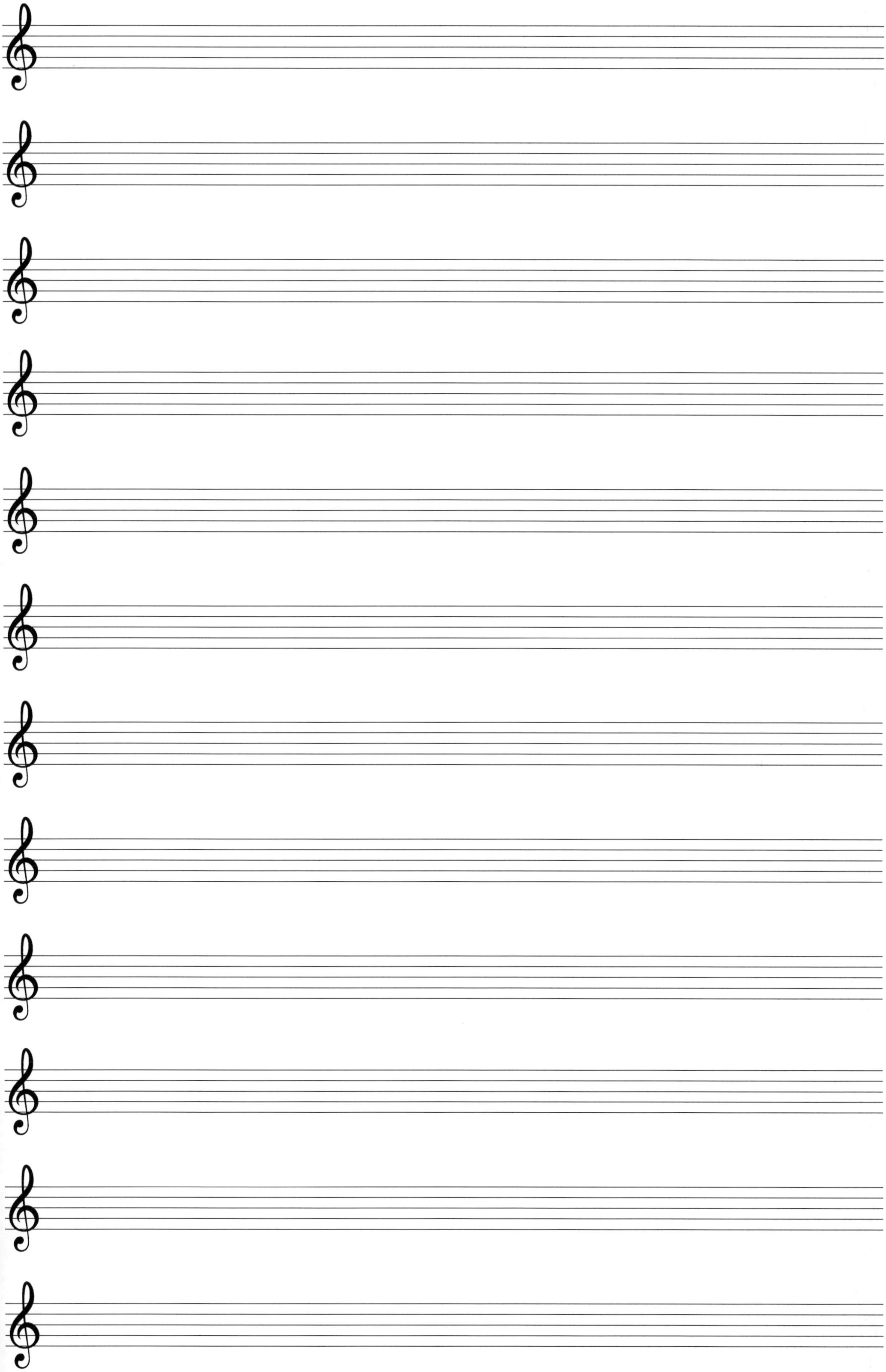

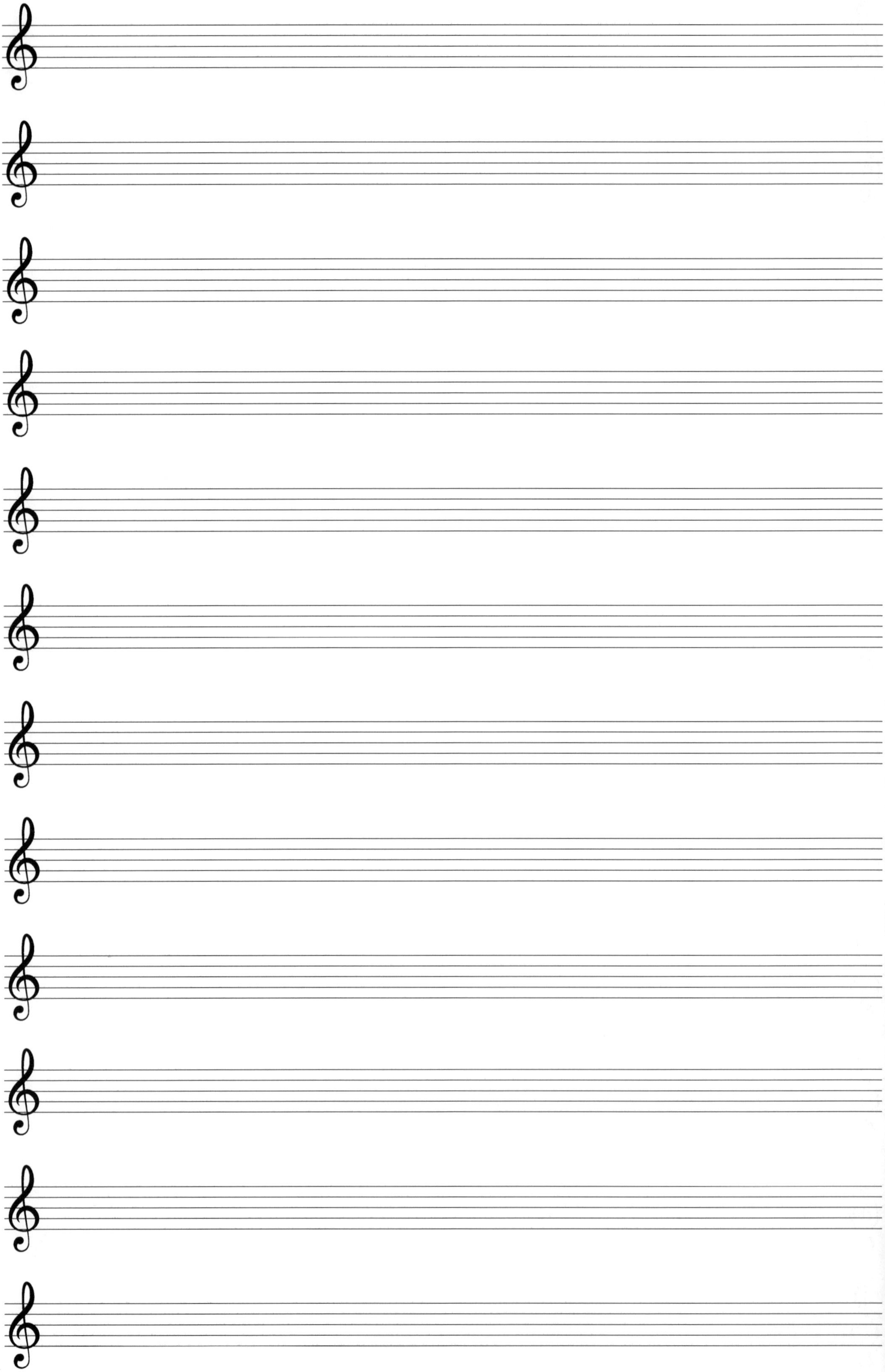

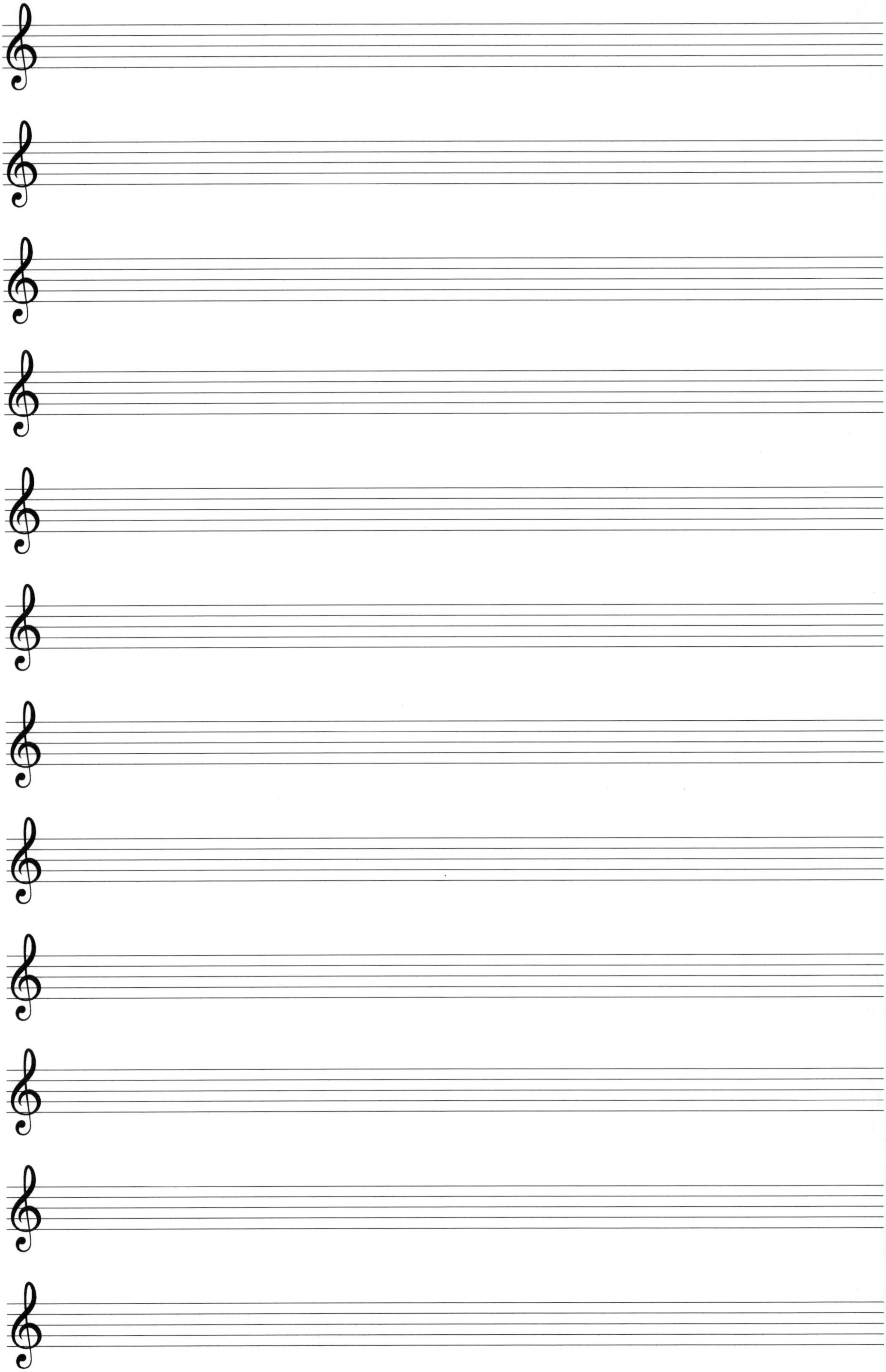

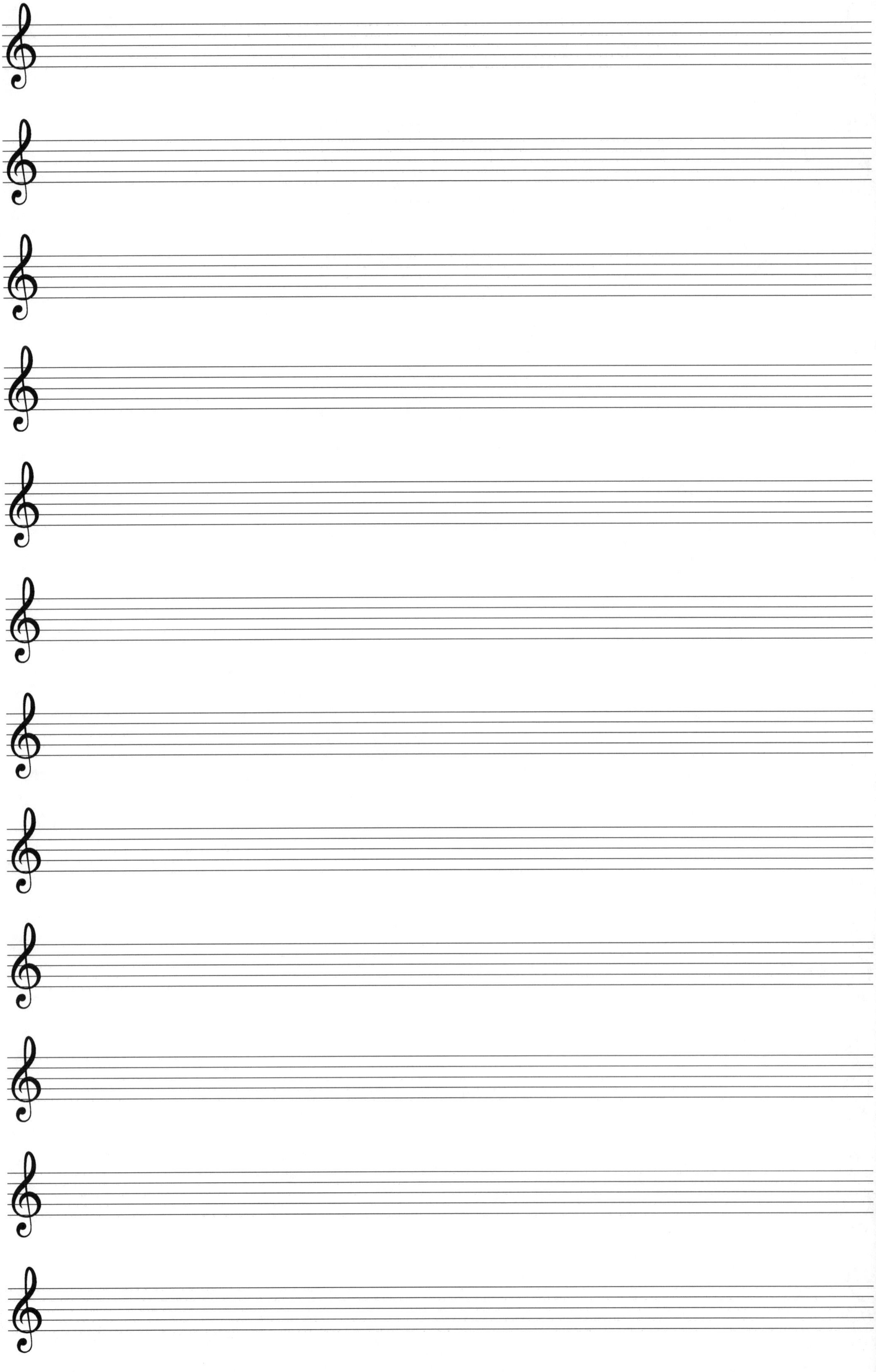

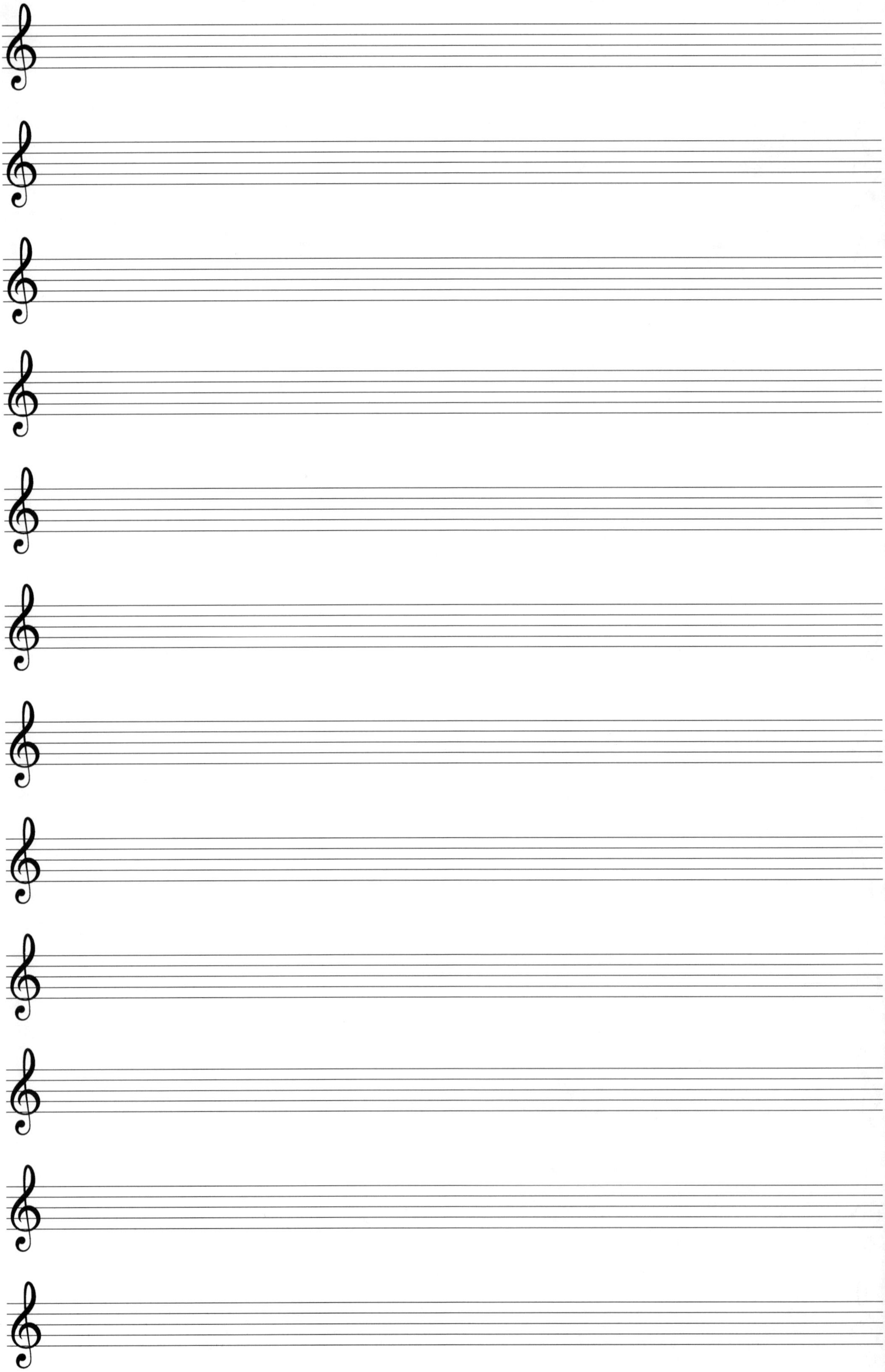

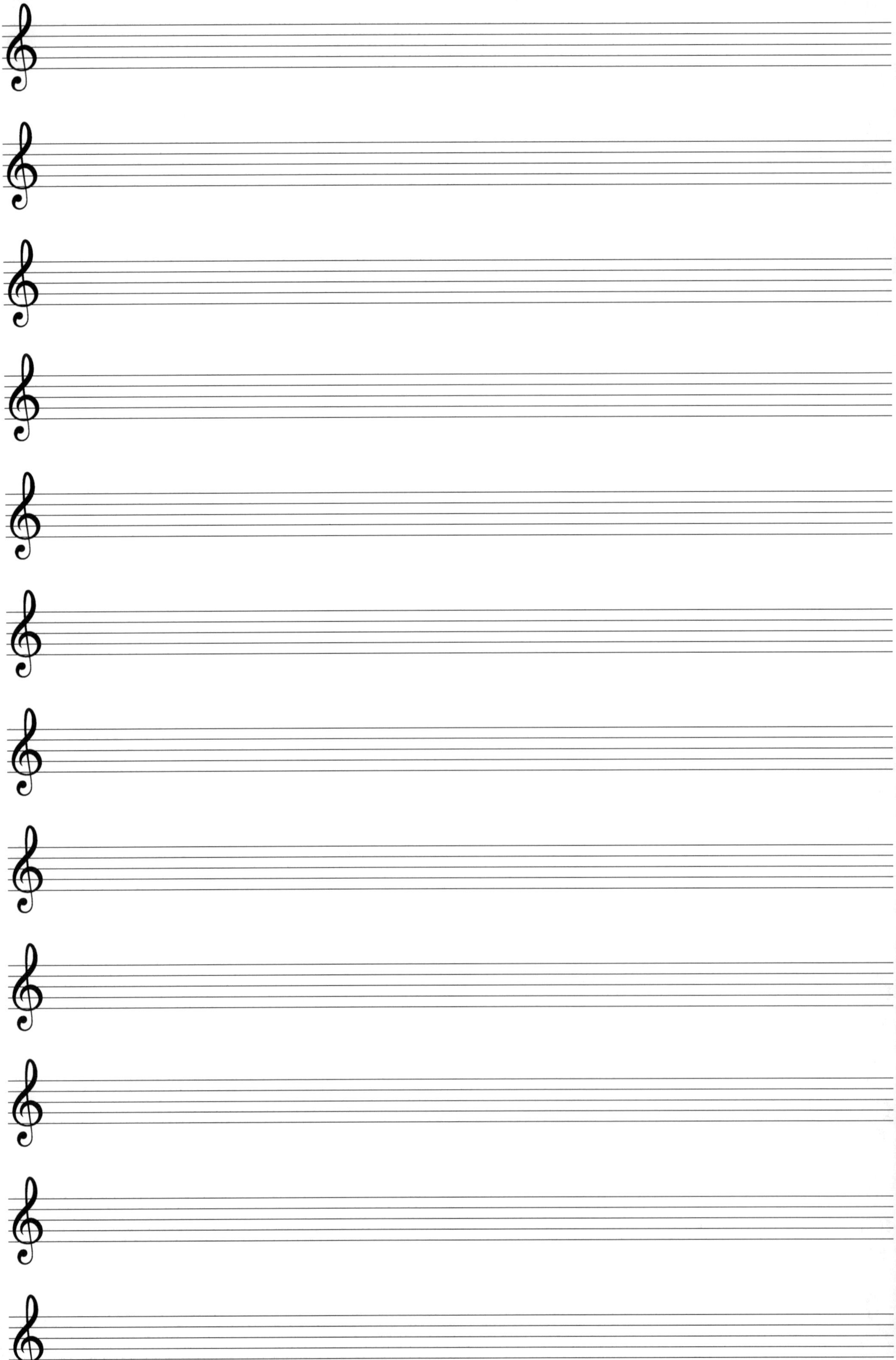

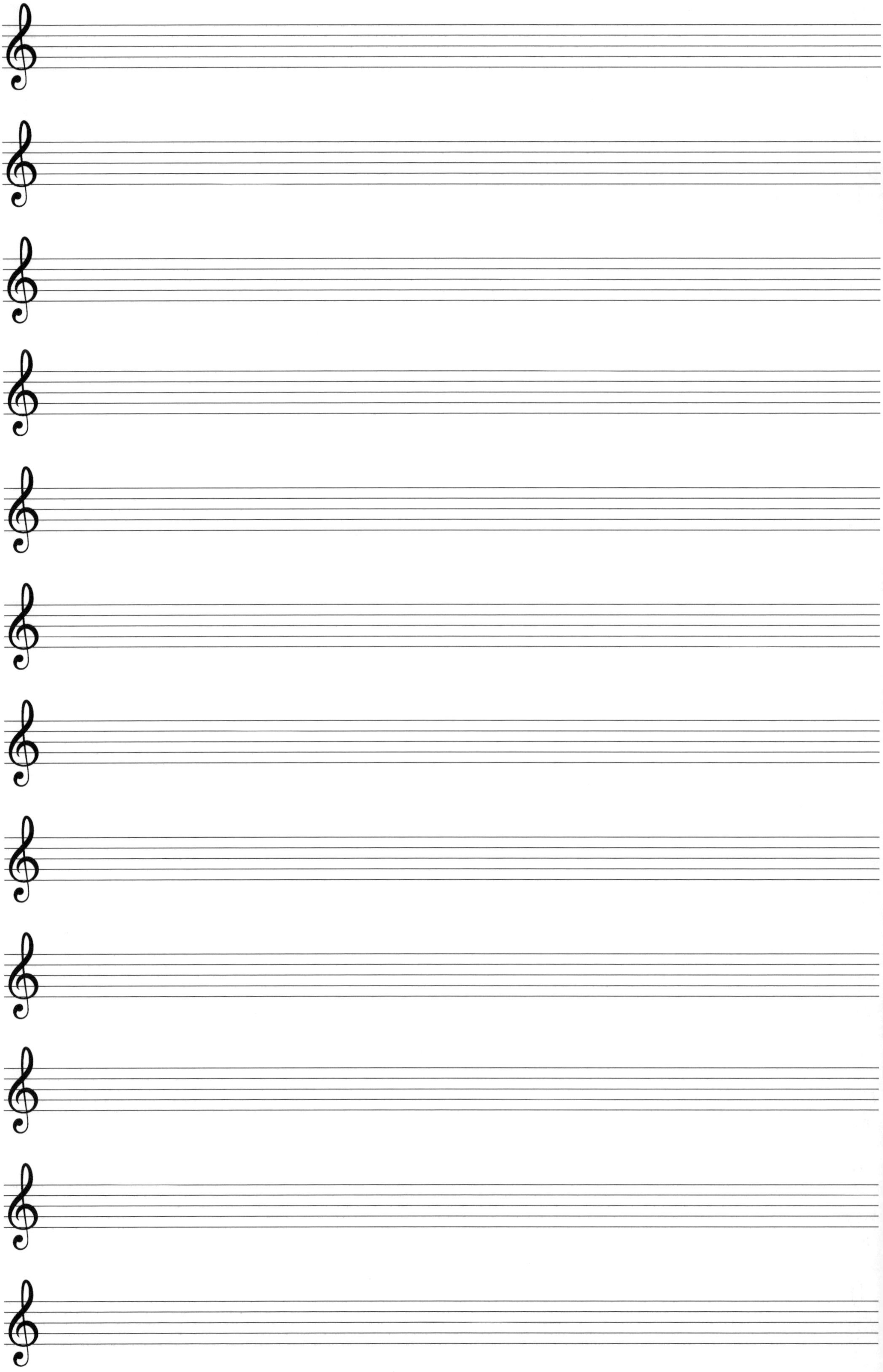

DigiPlus

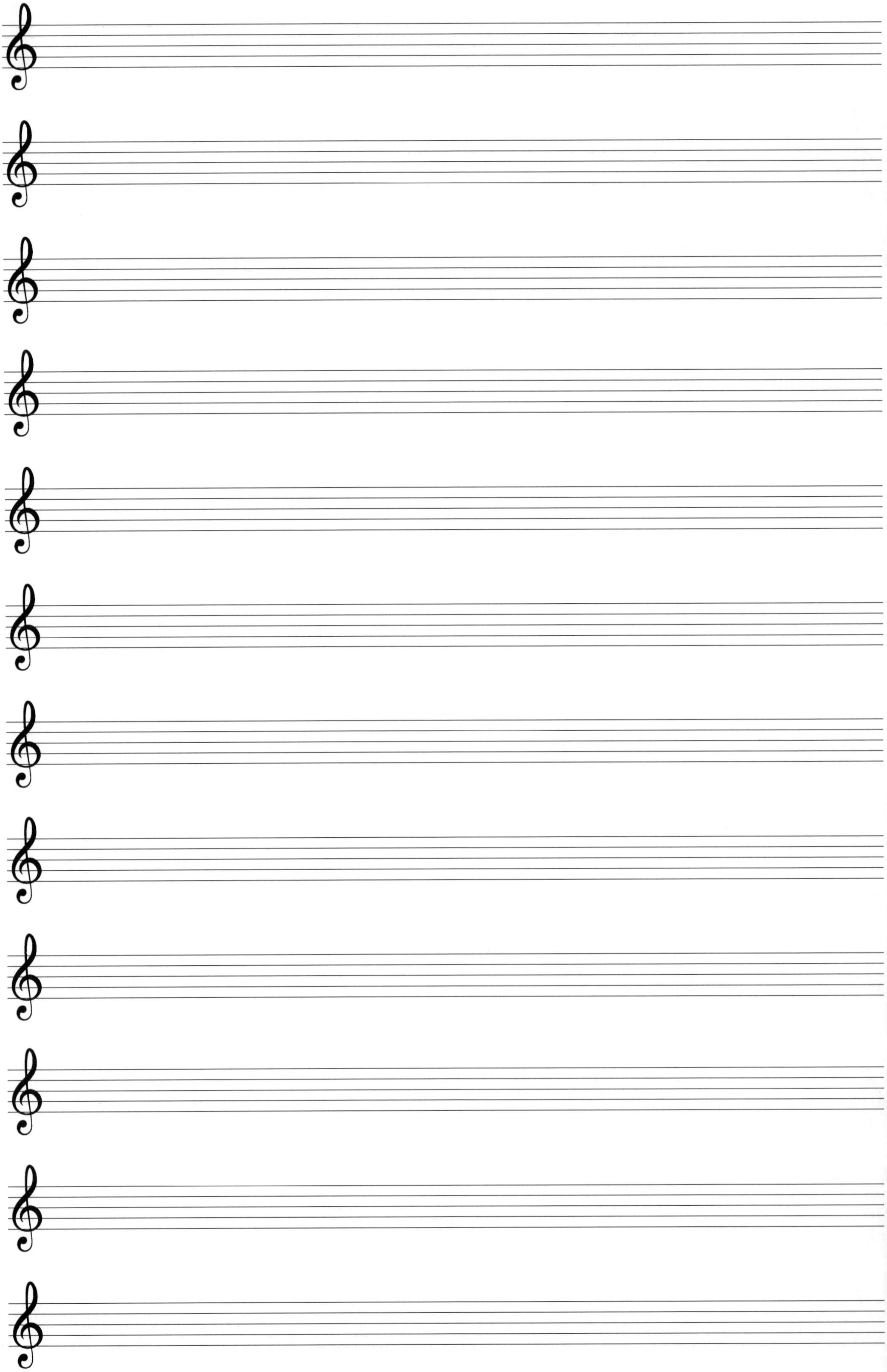

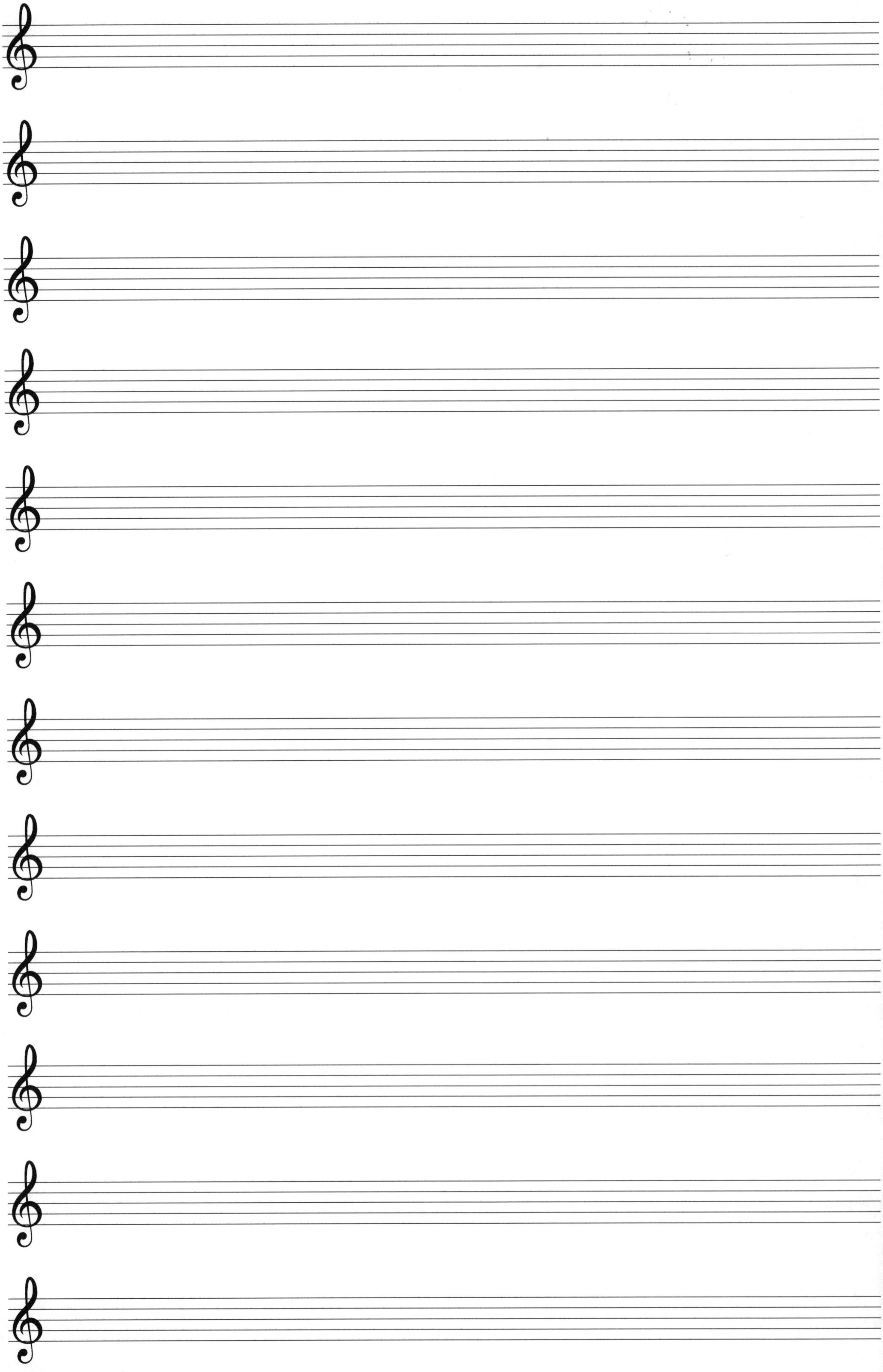

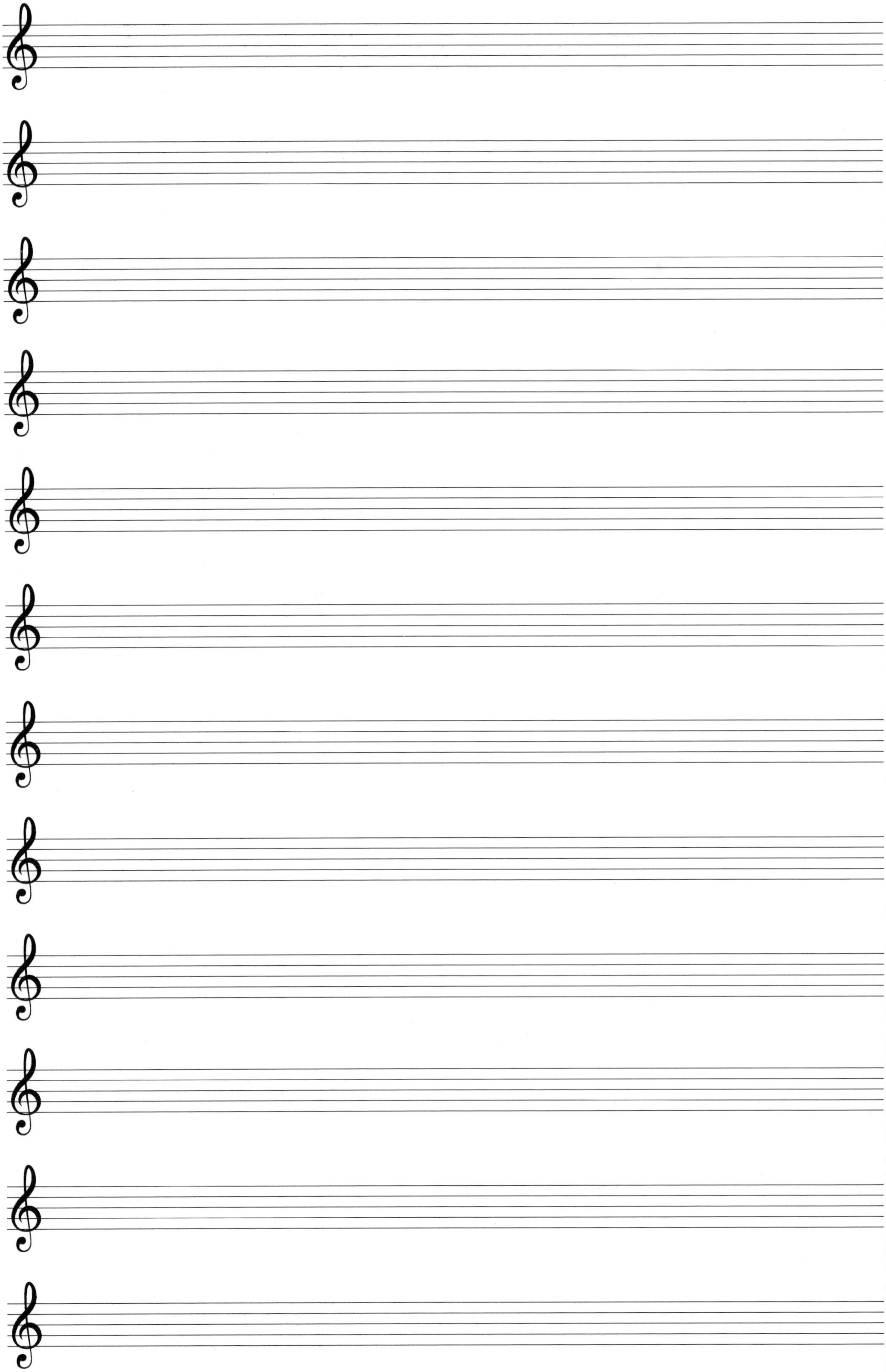

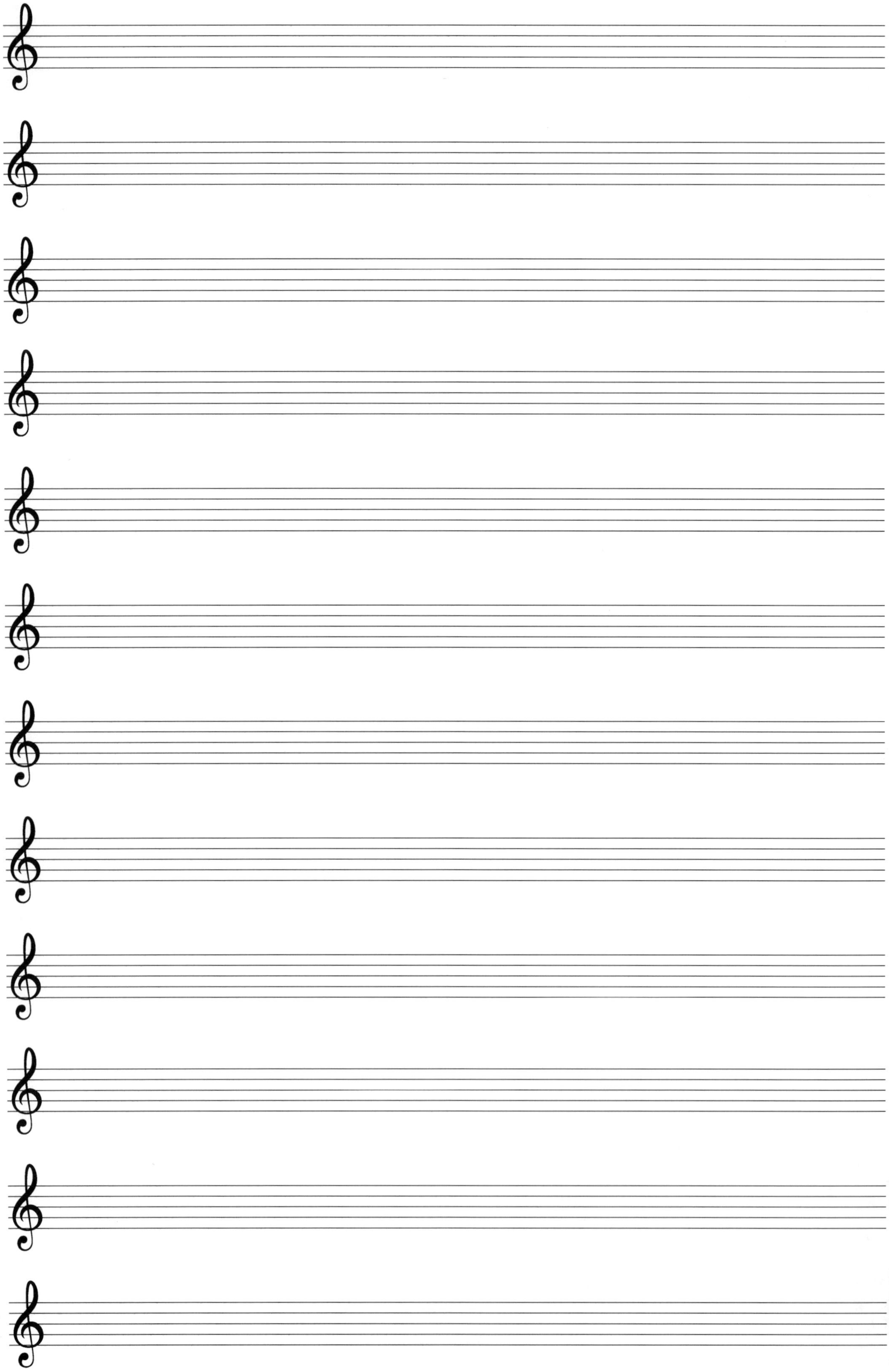

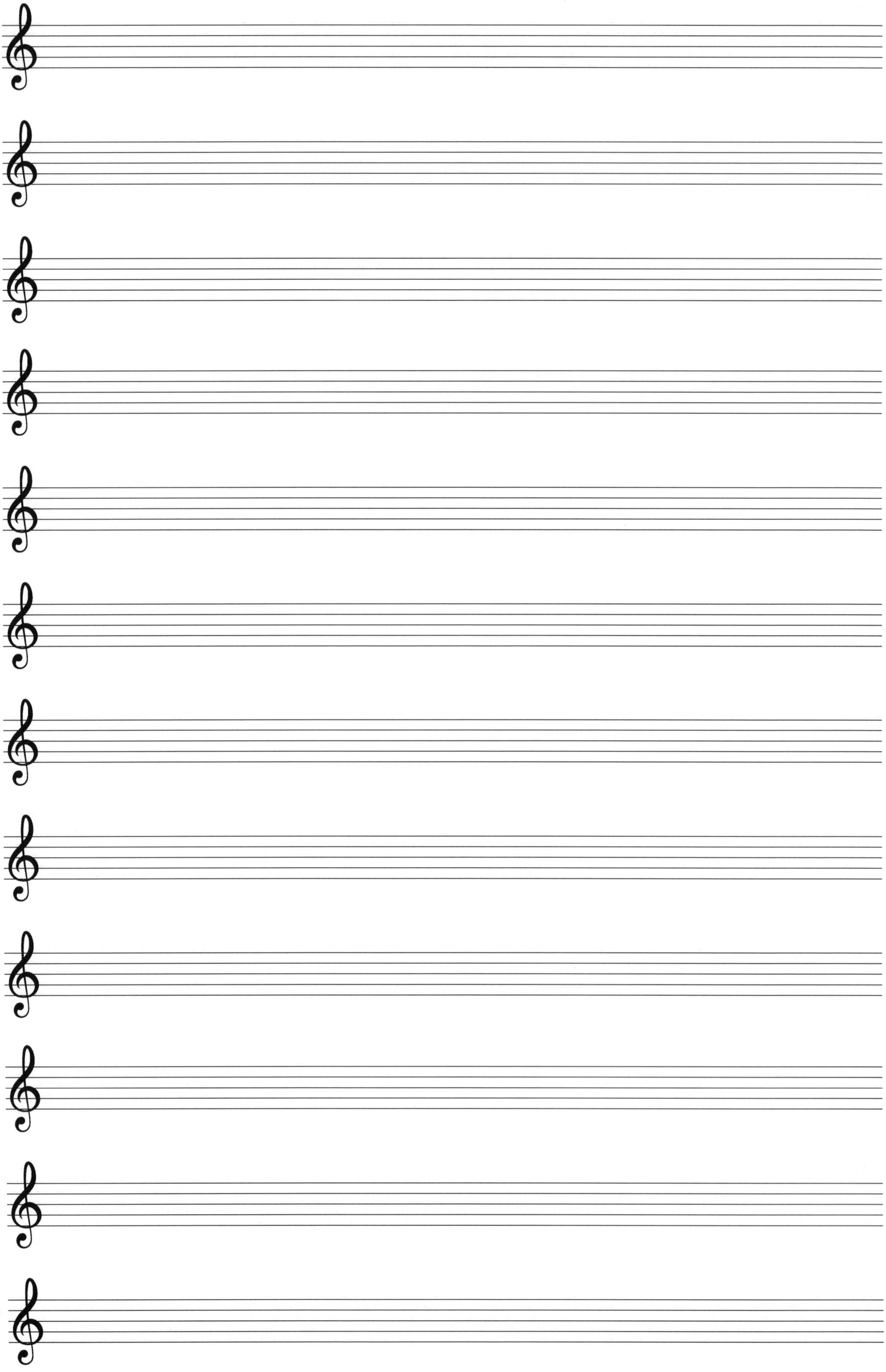

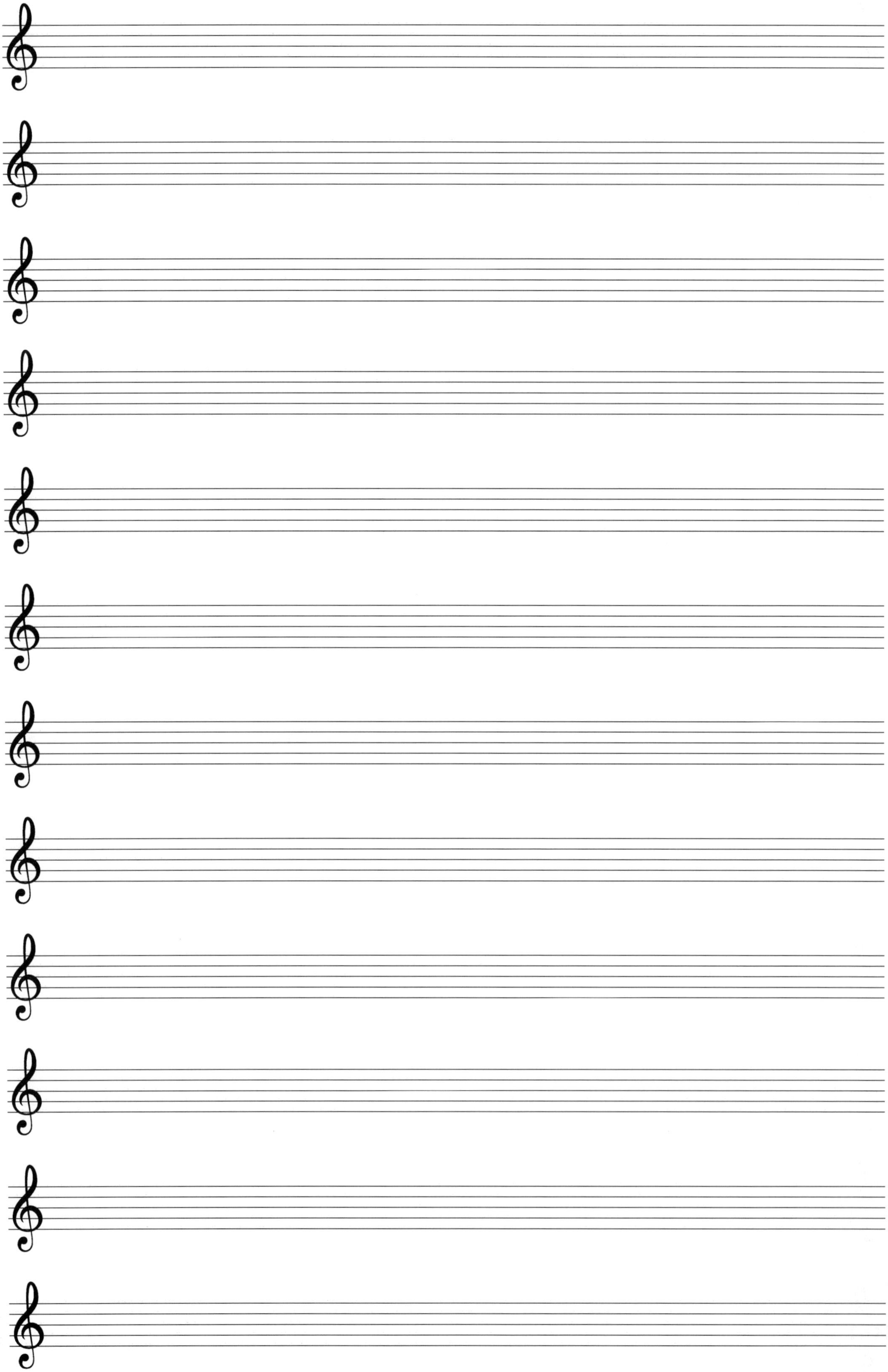

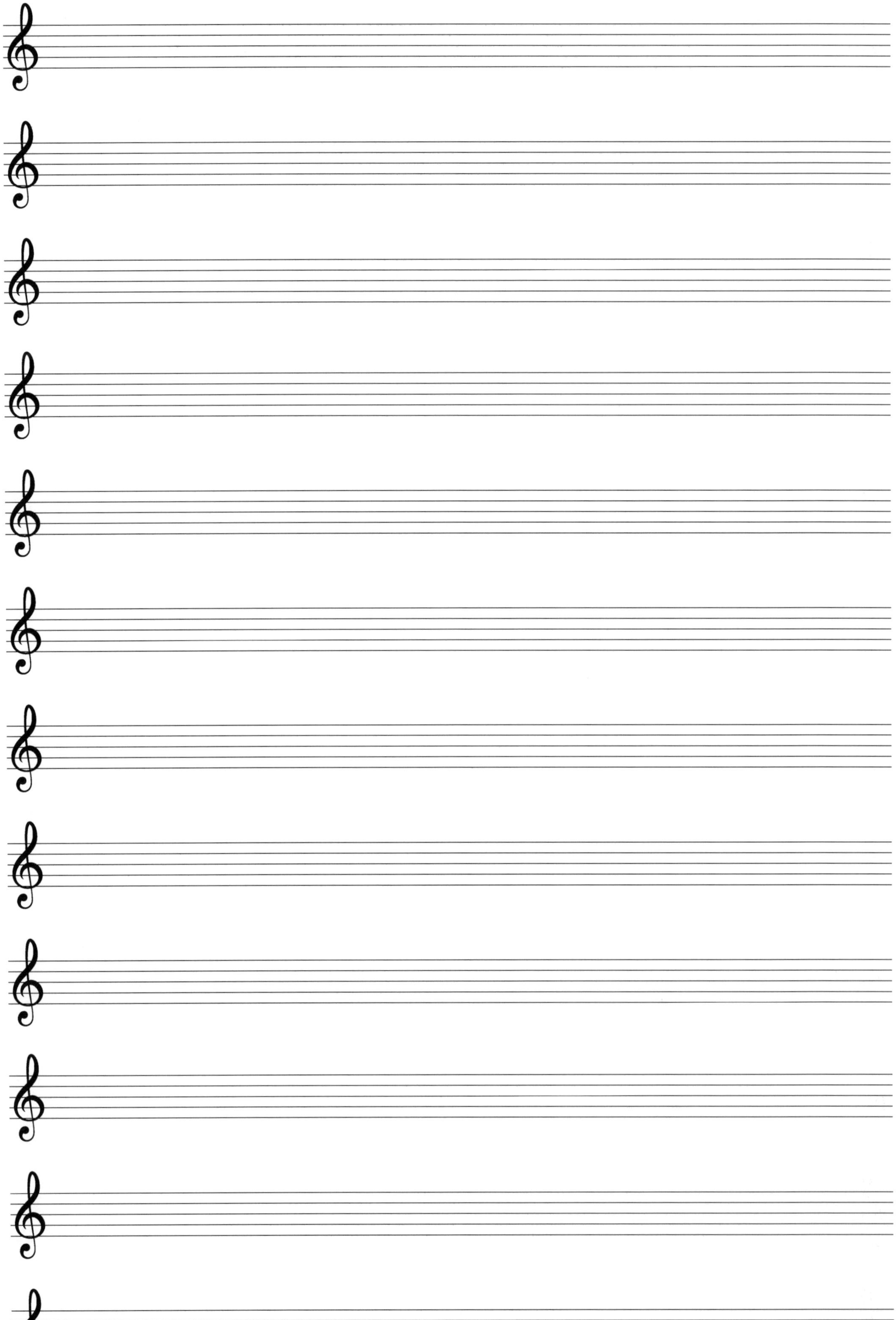

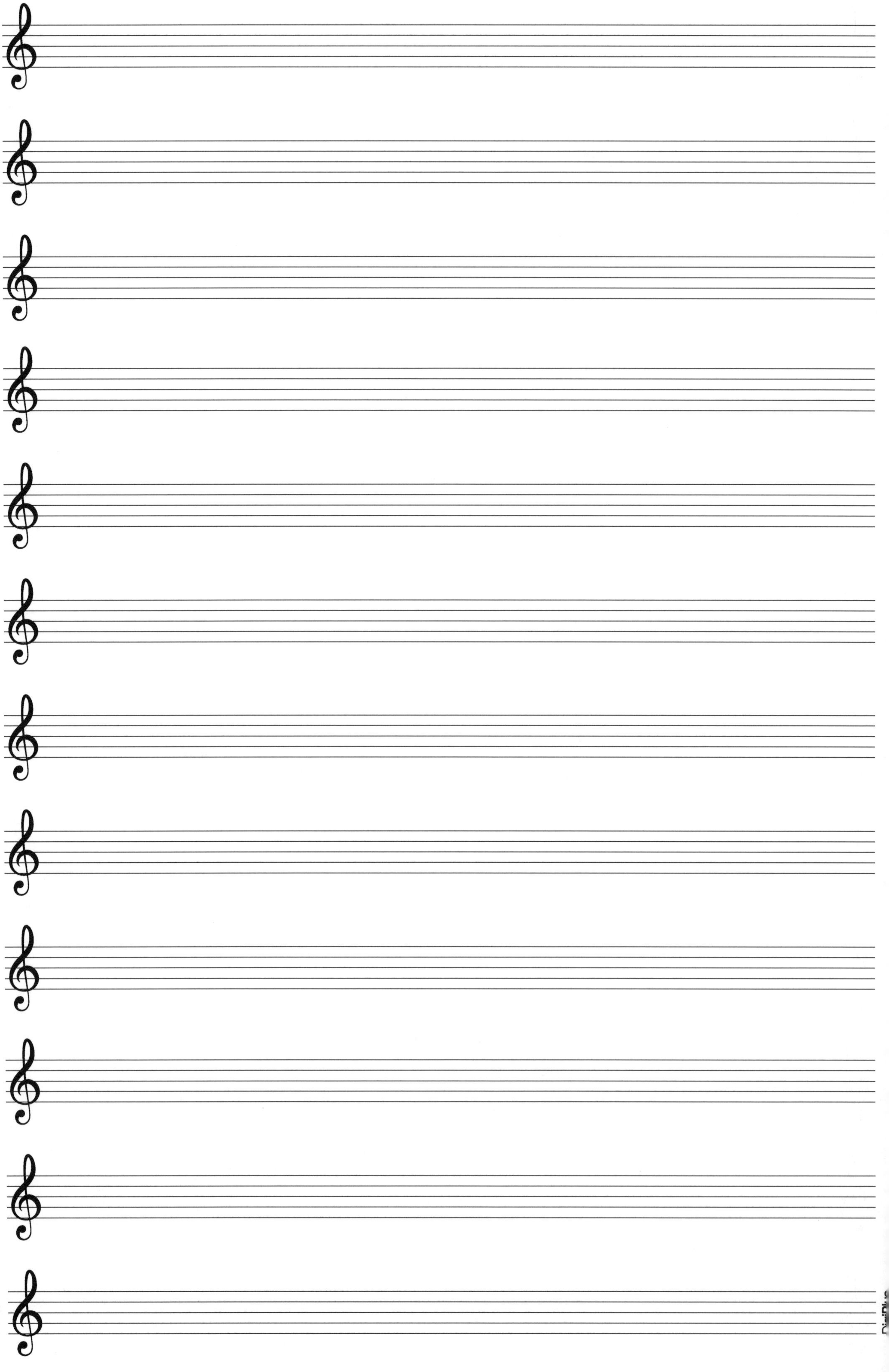

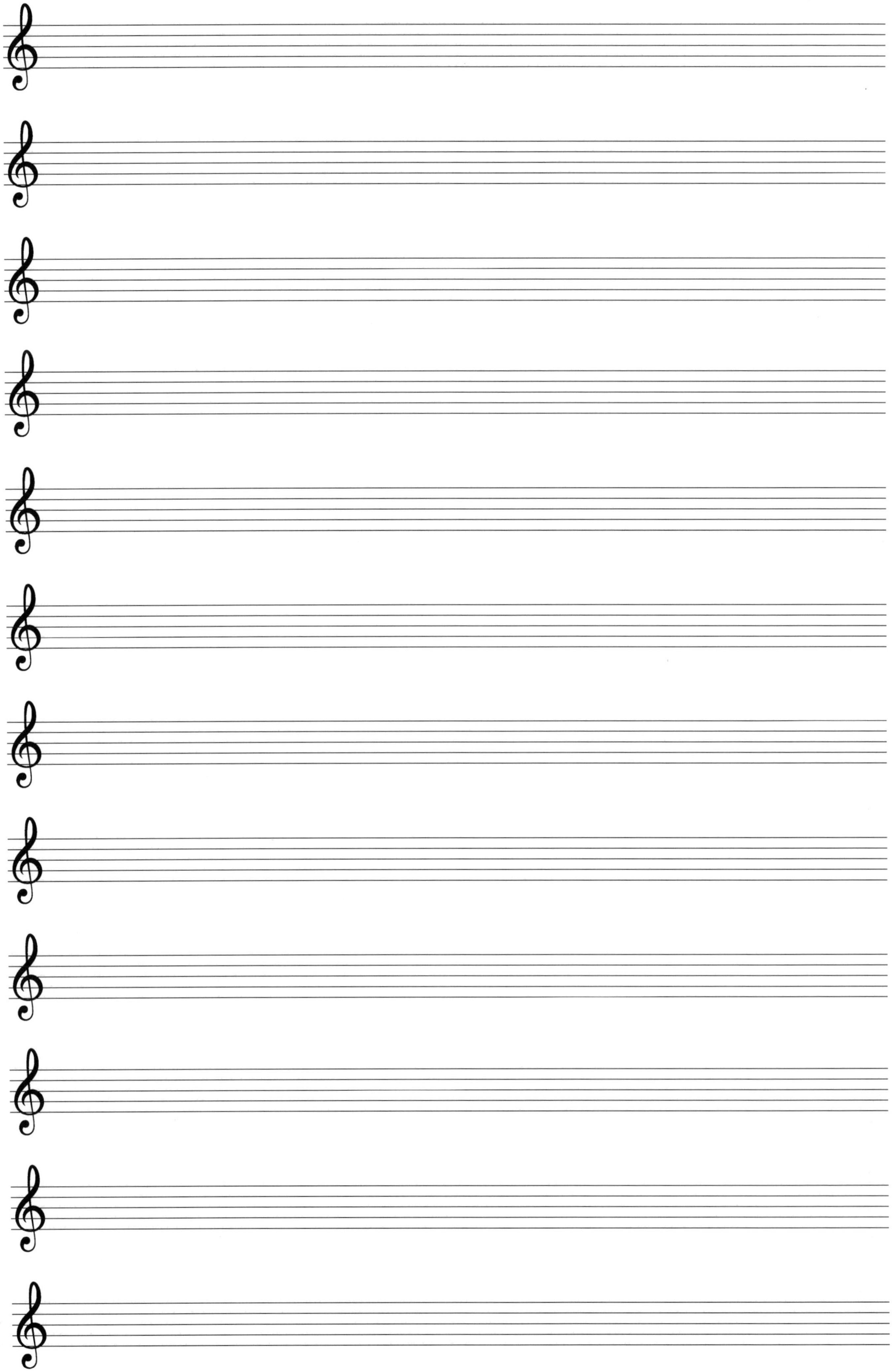

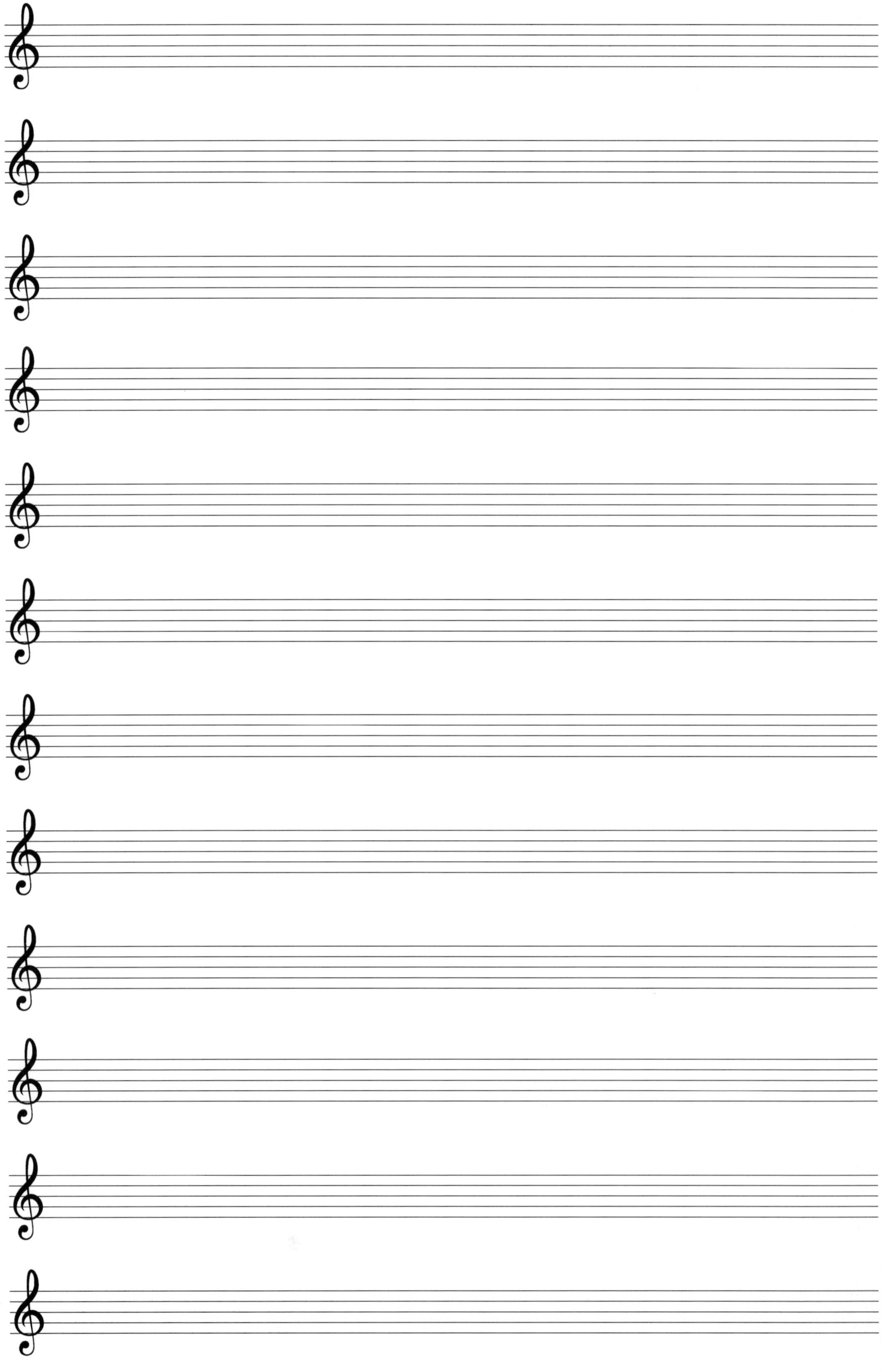

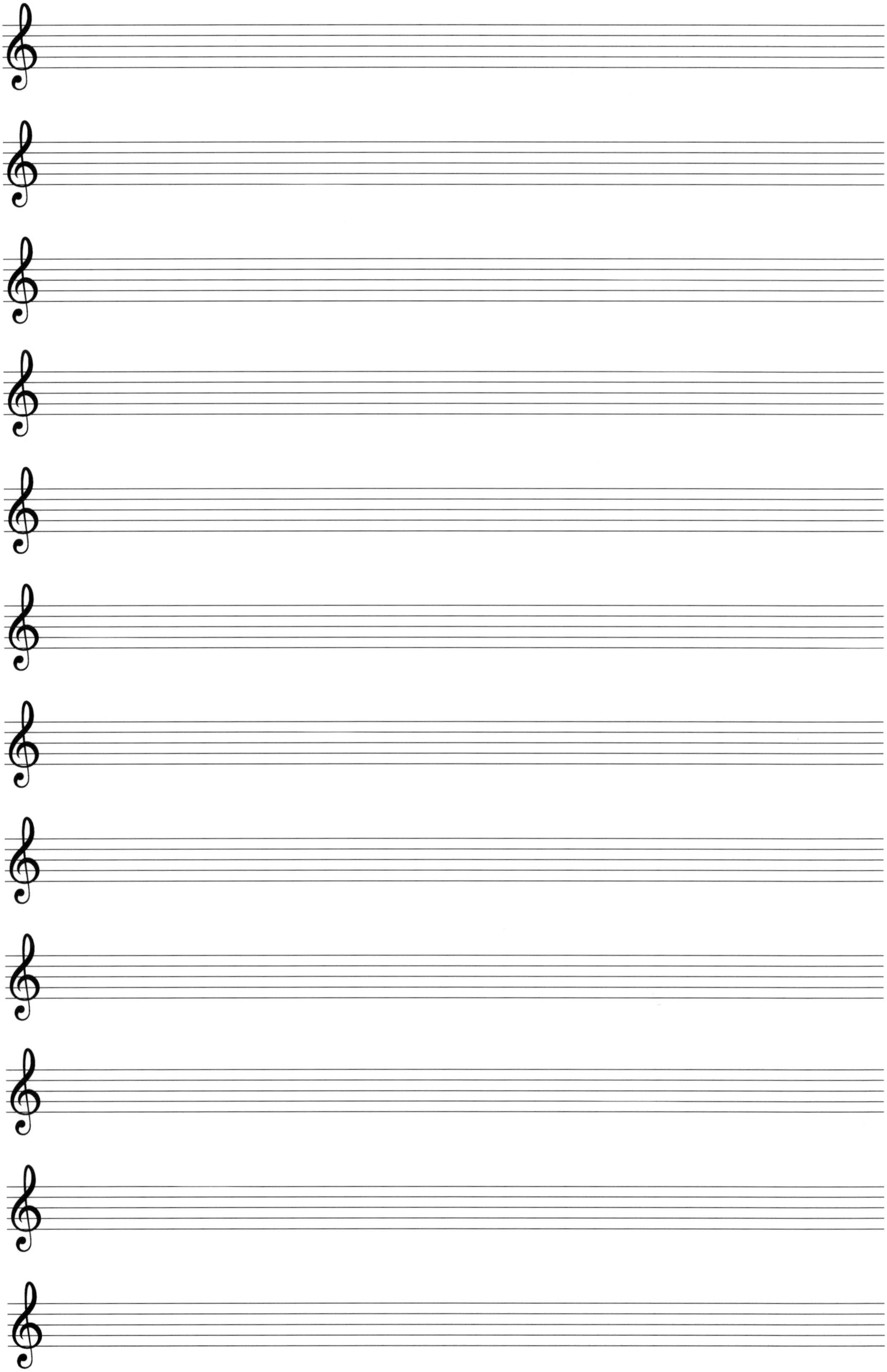

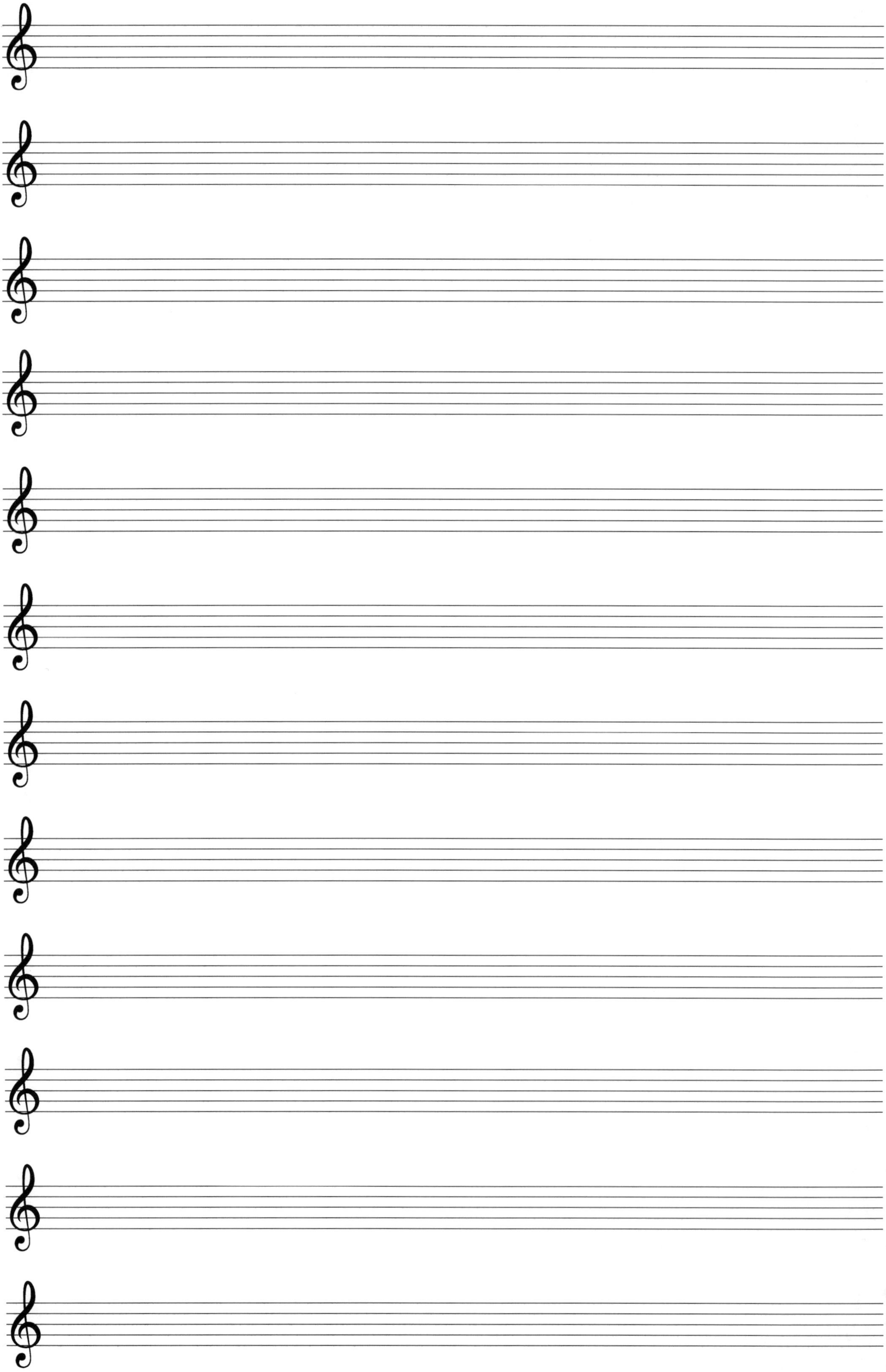

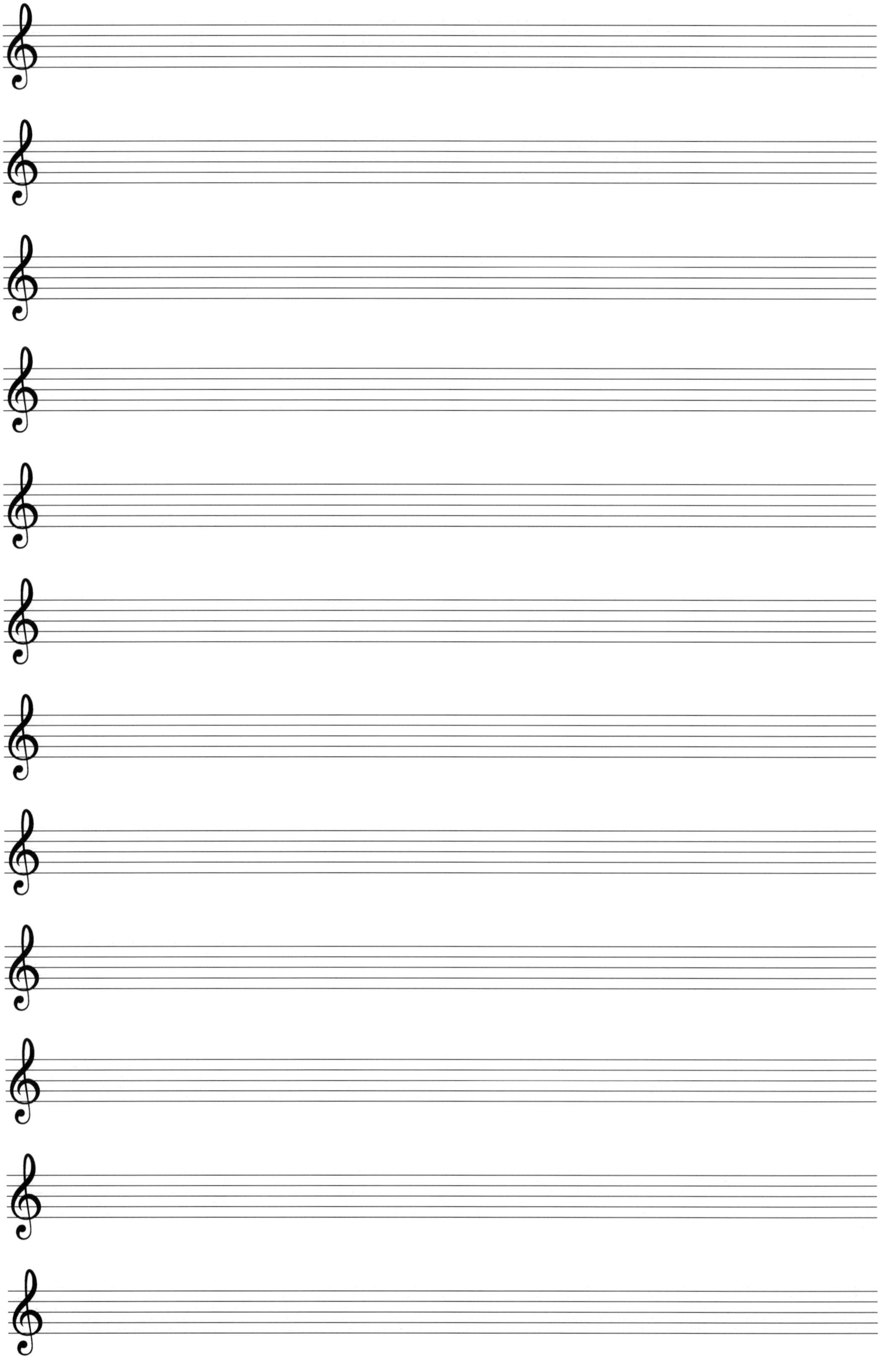

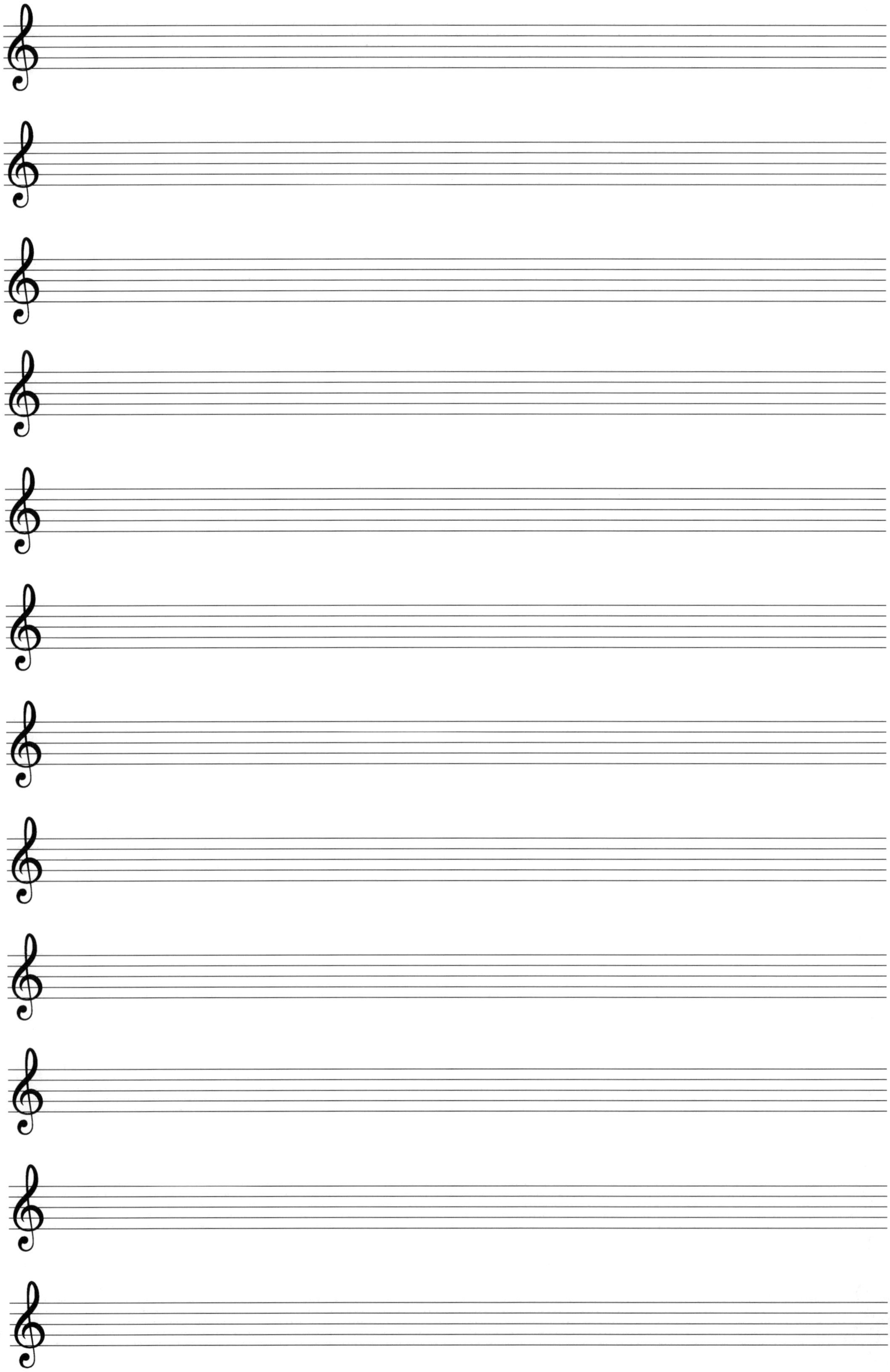

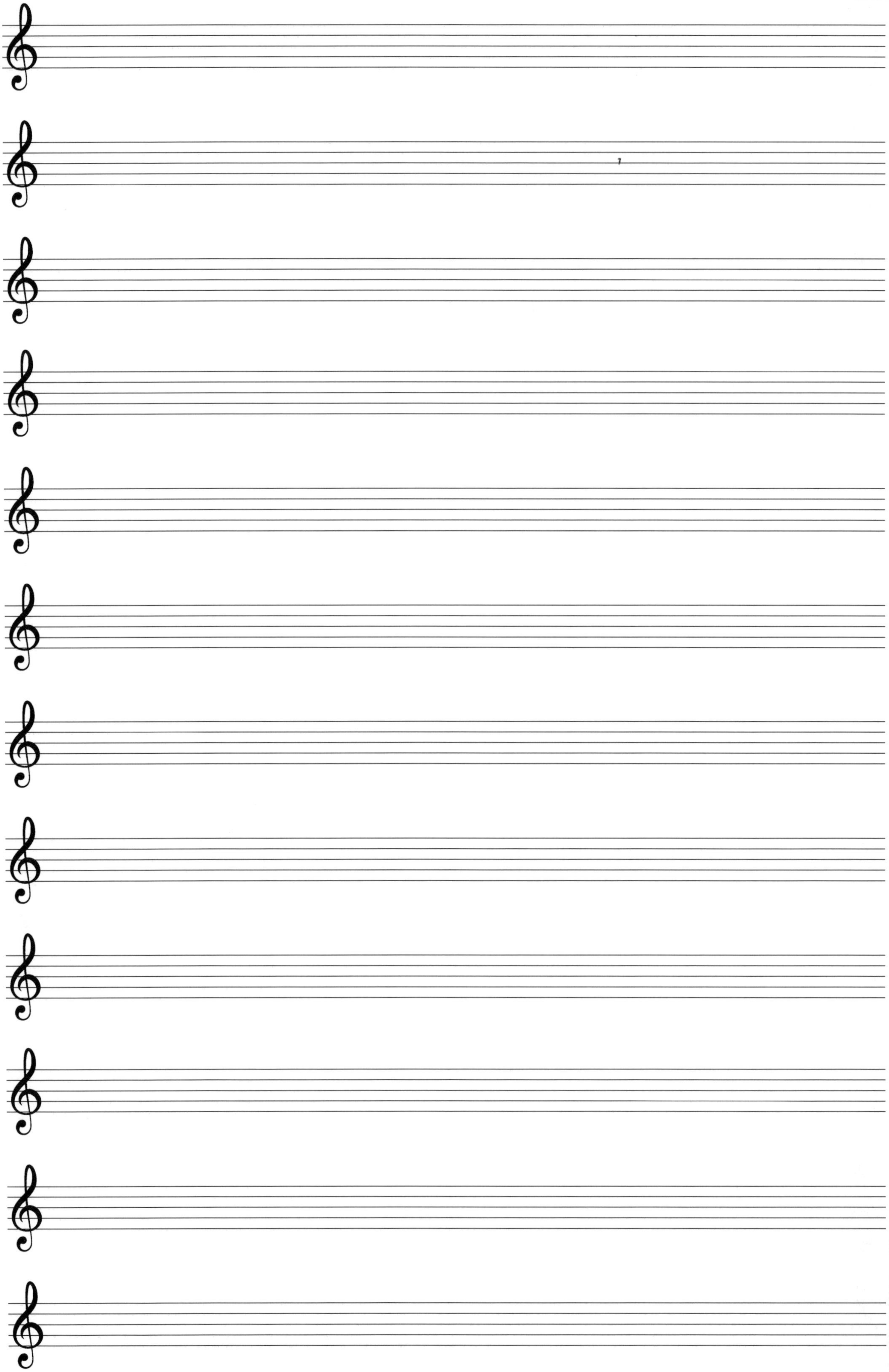

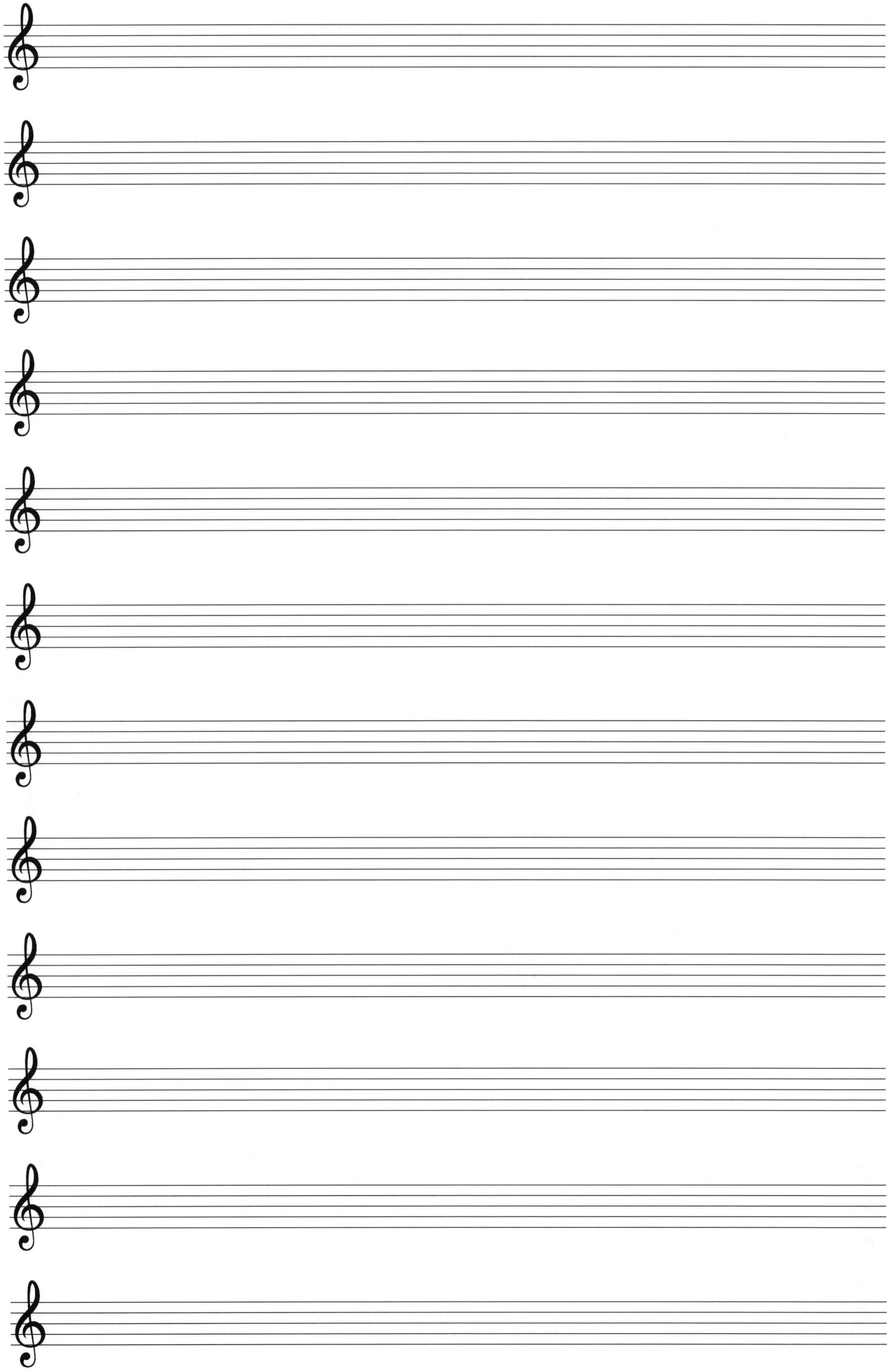

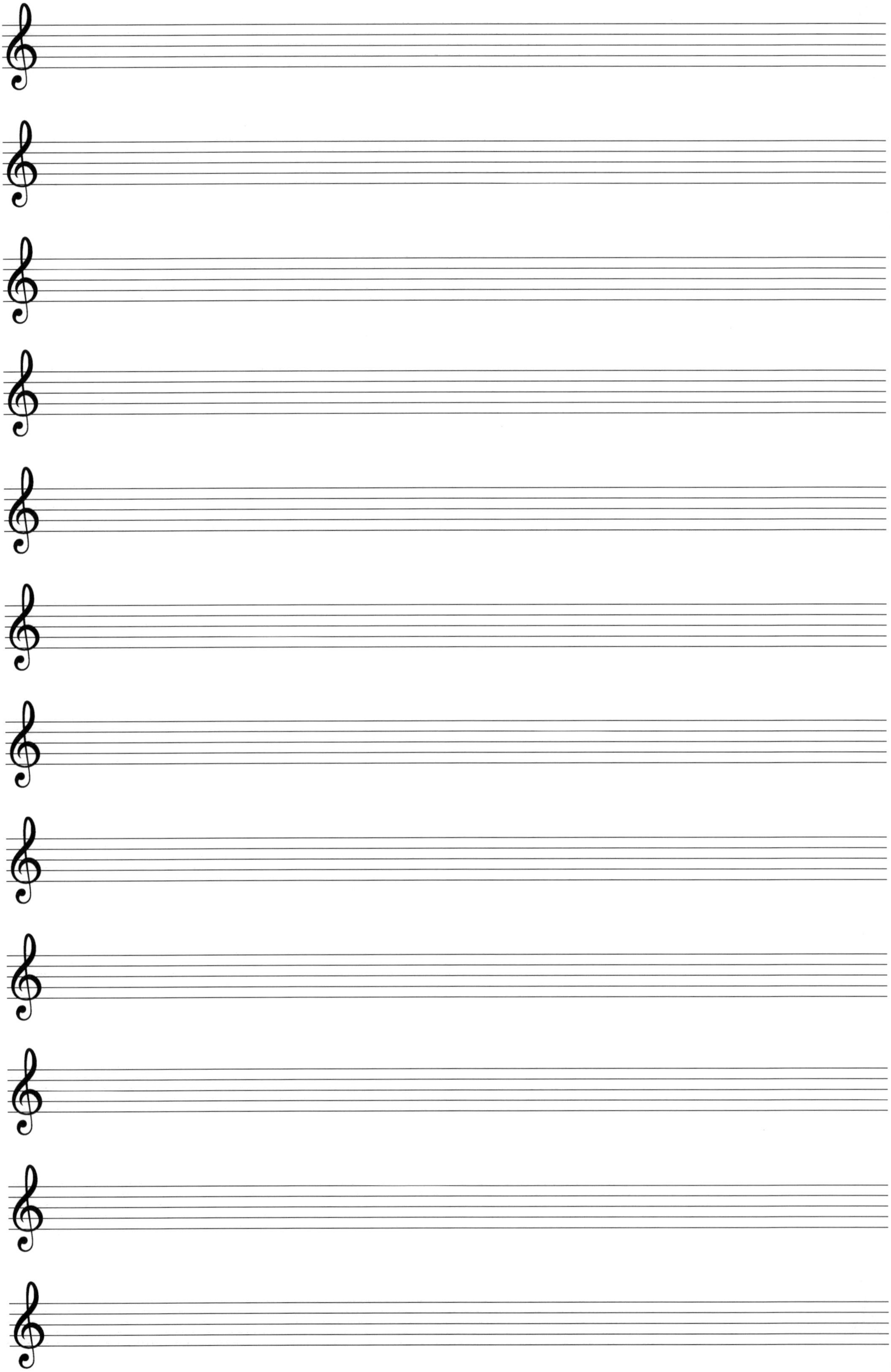

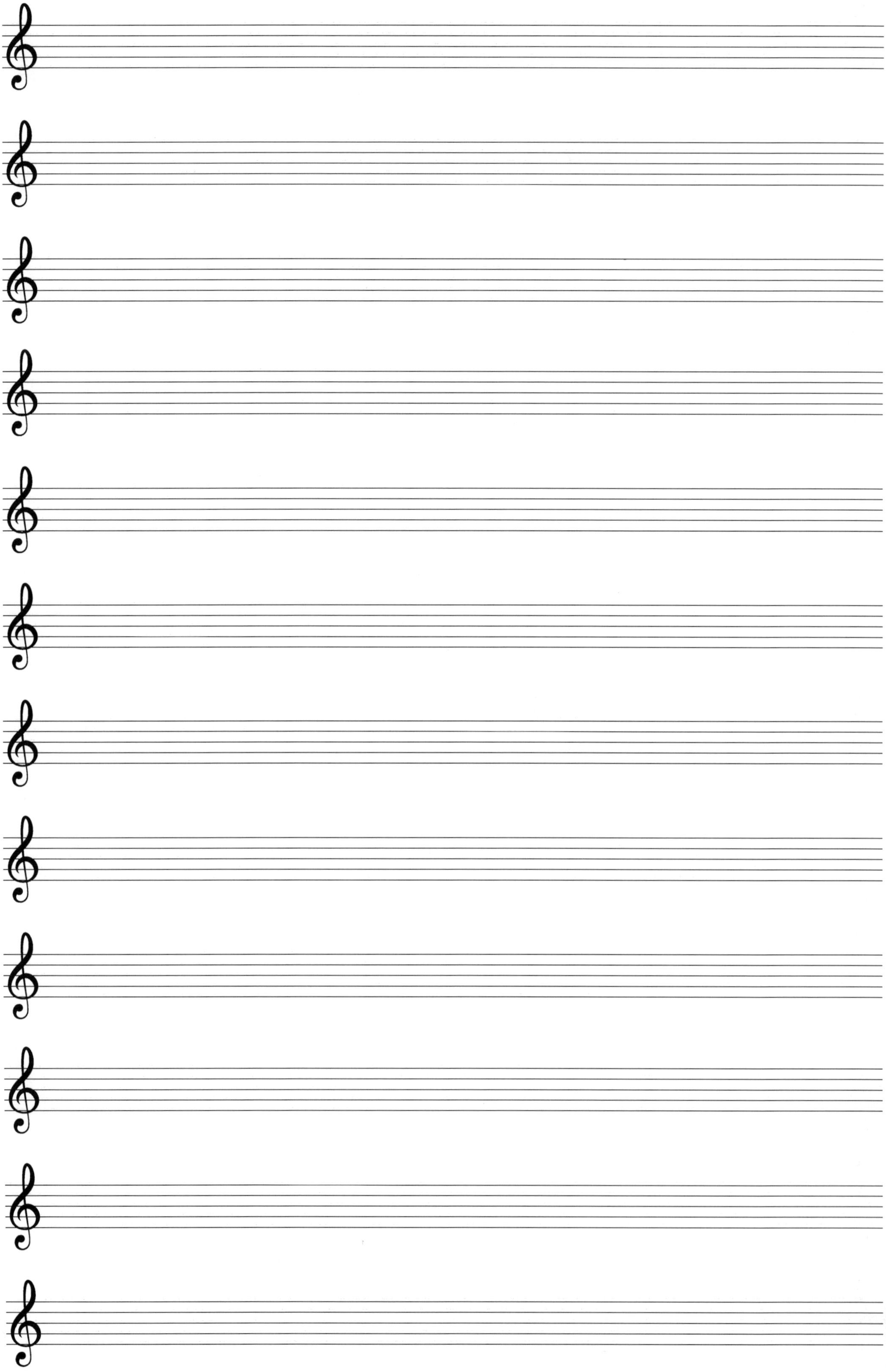

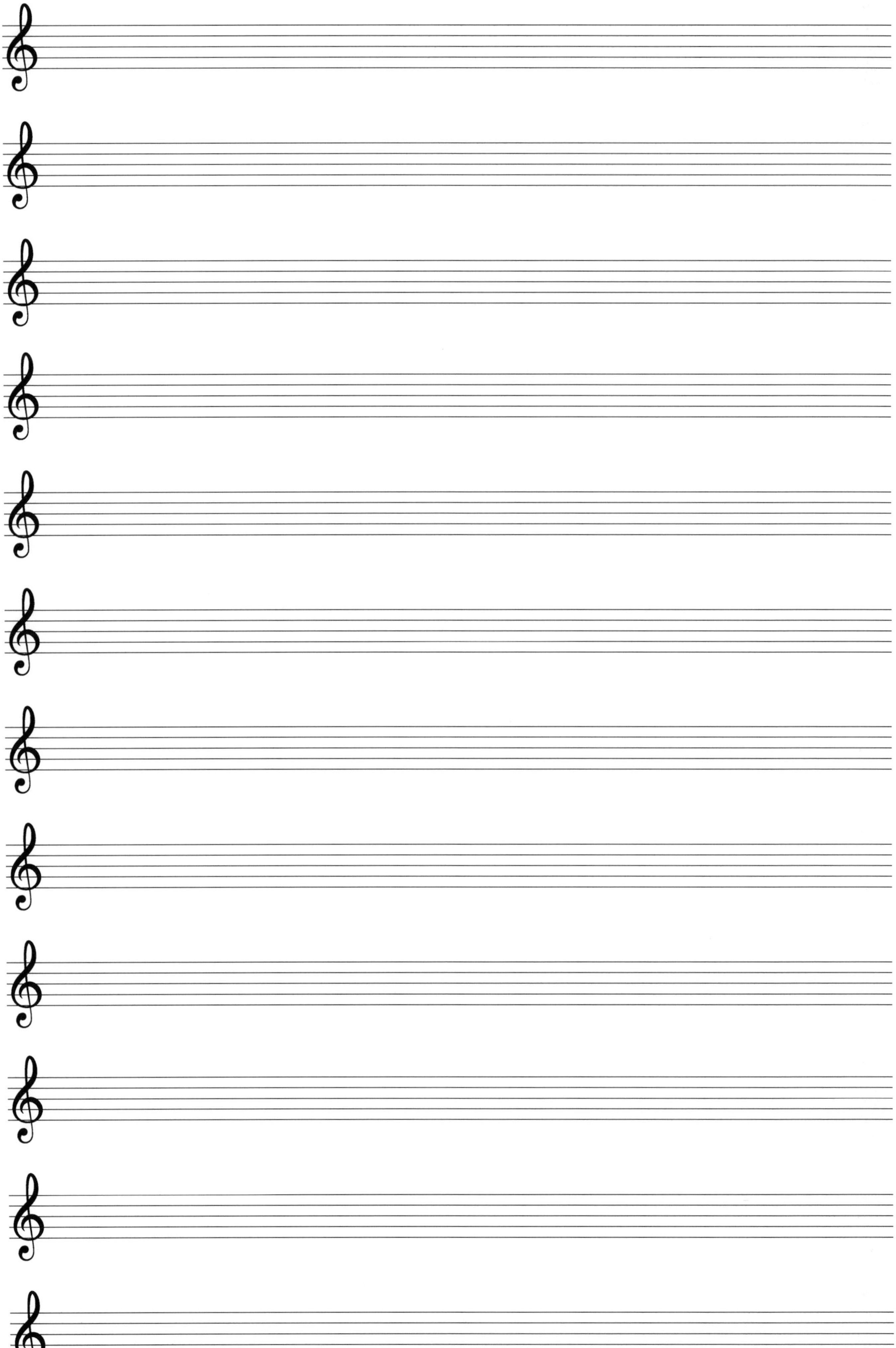

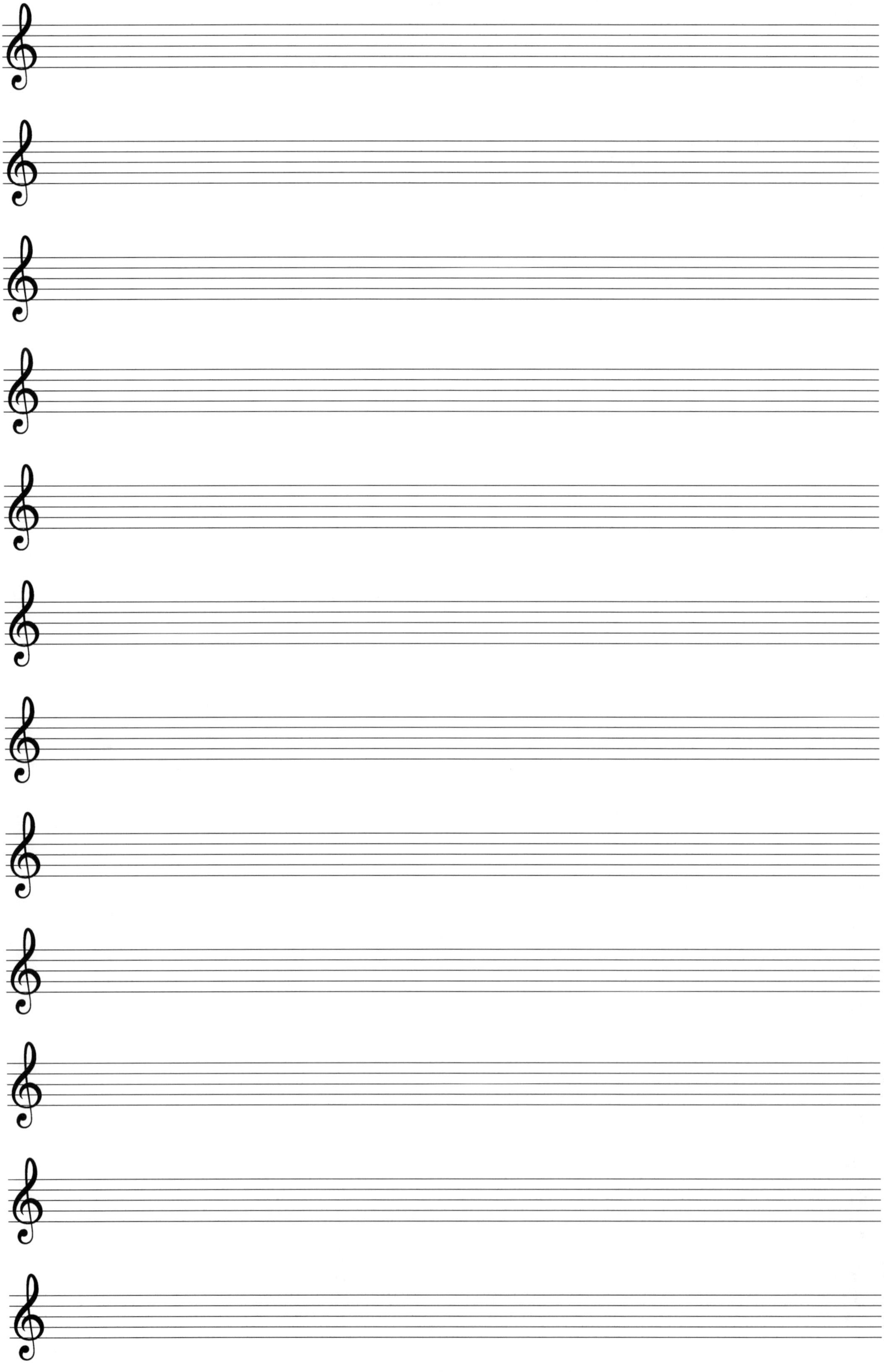

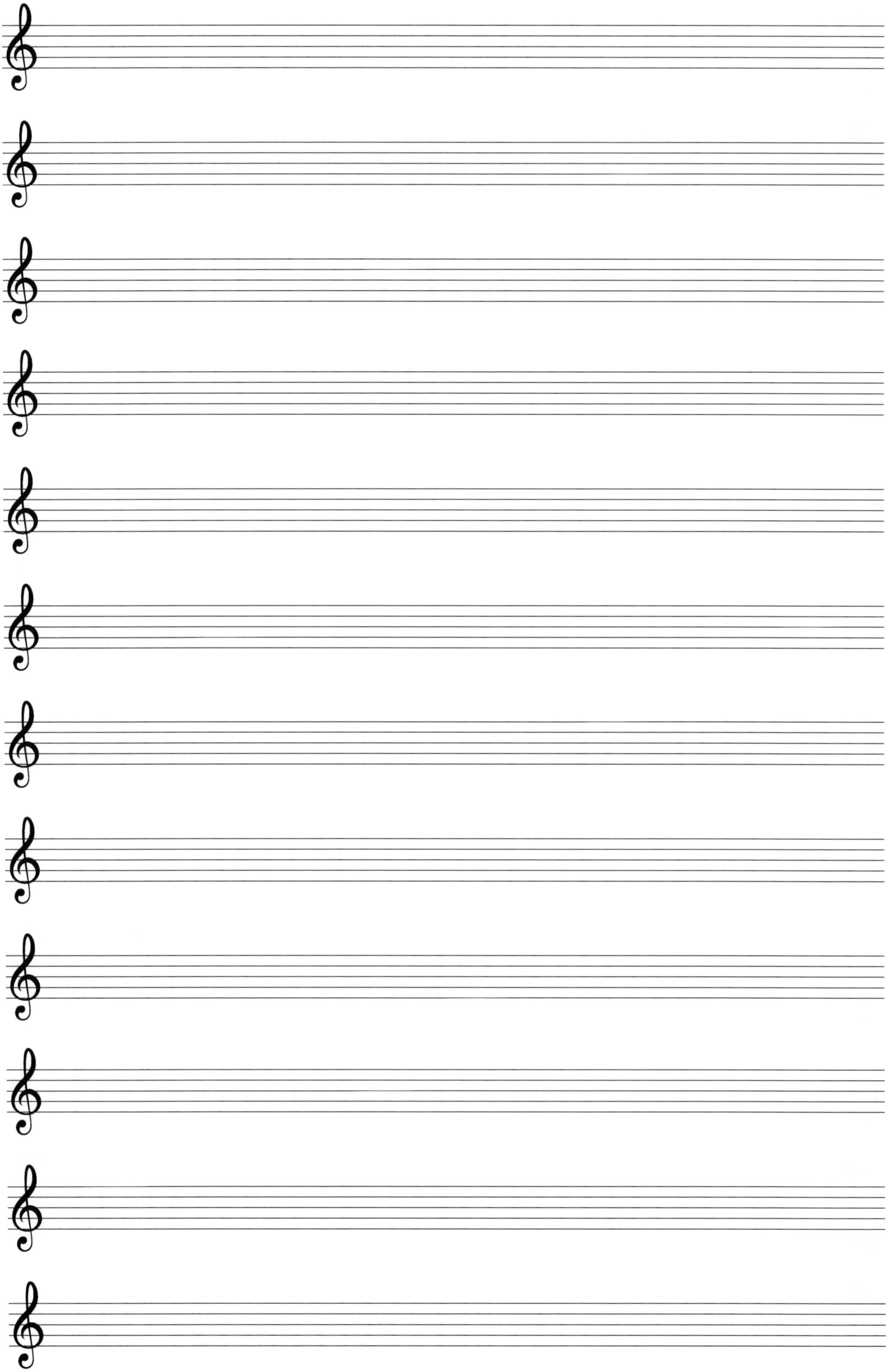

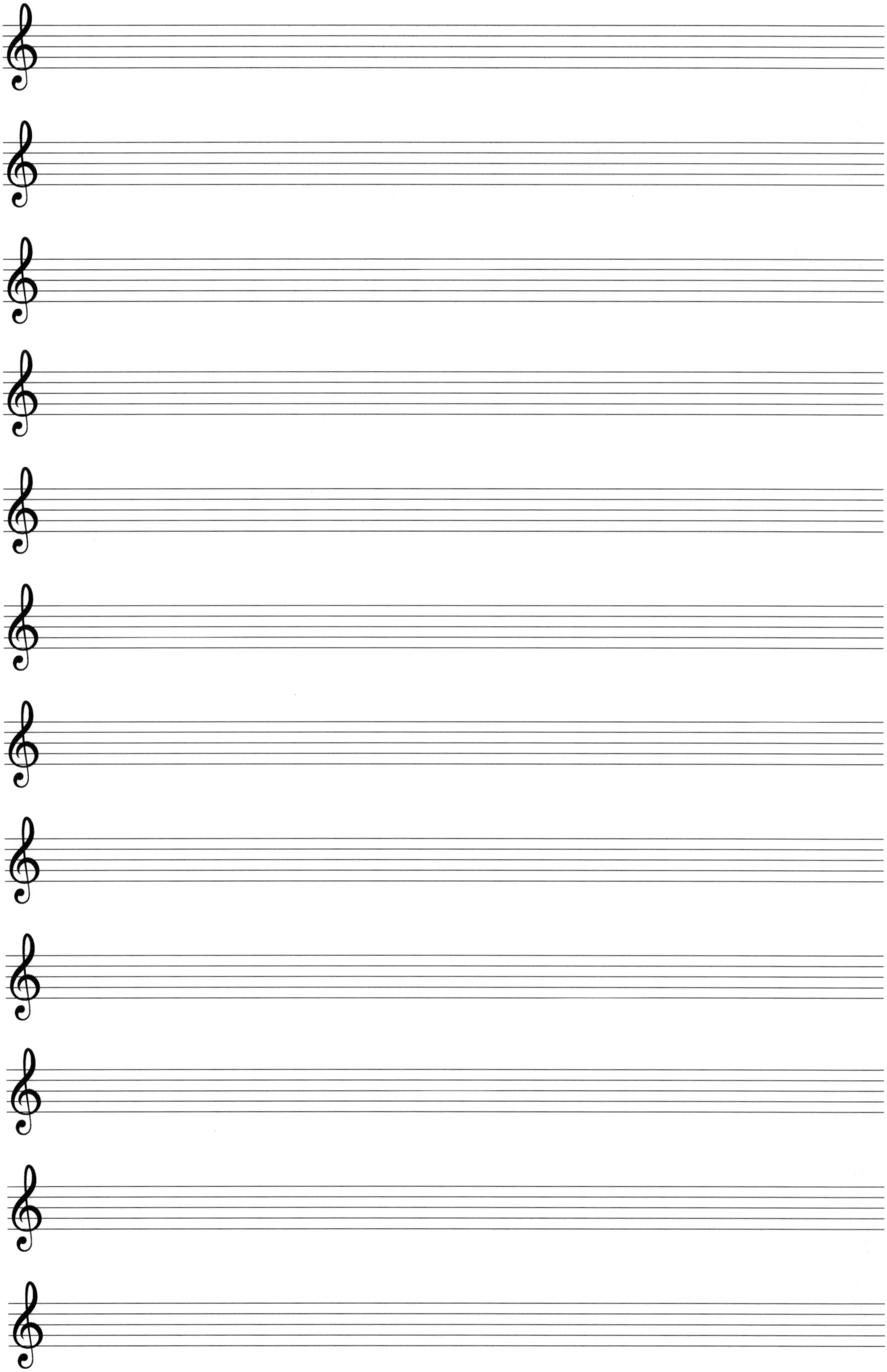

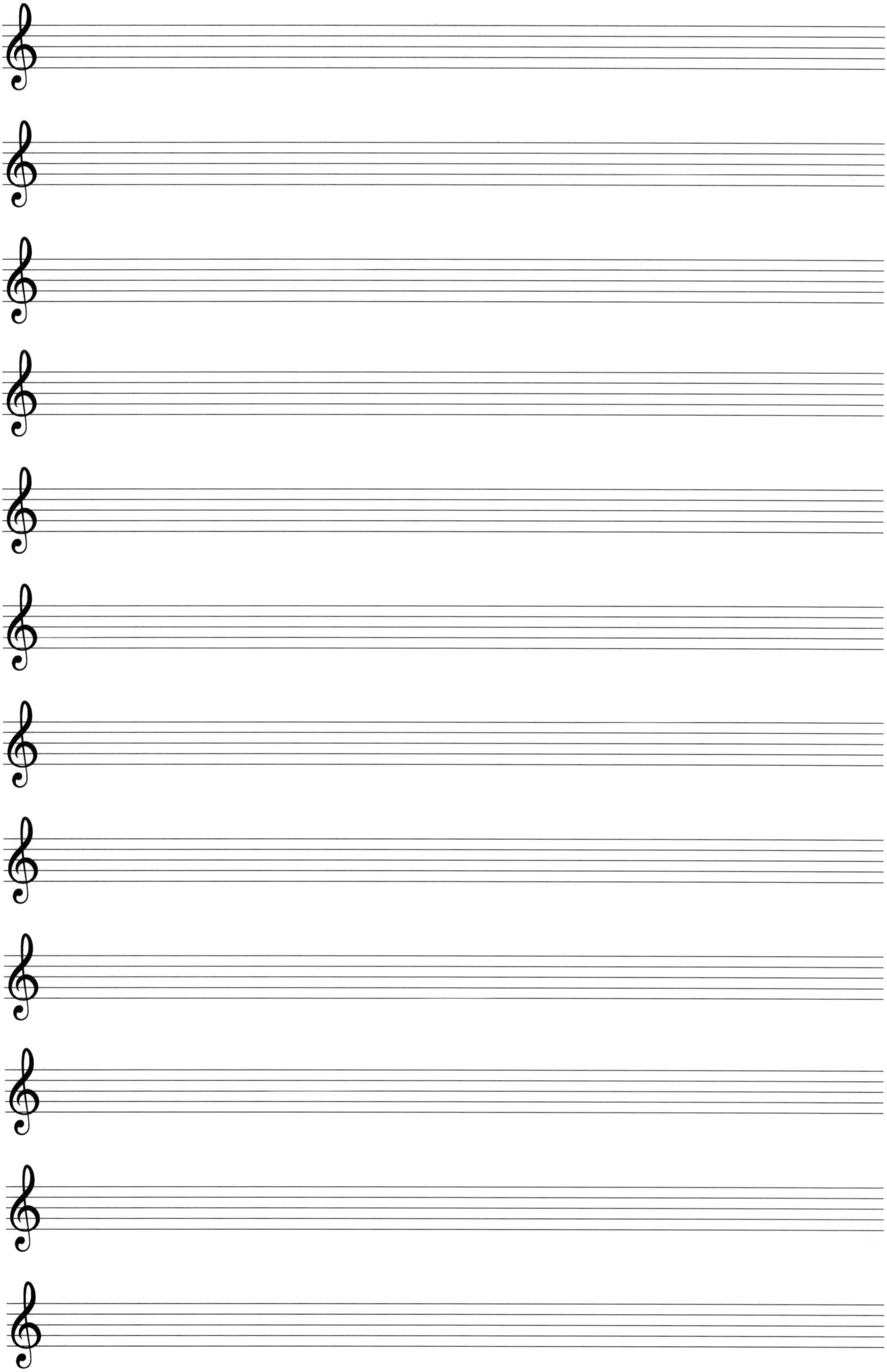

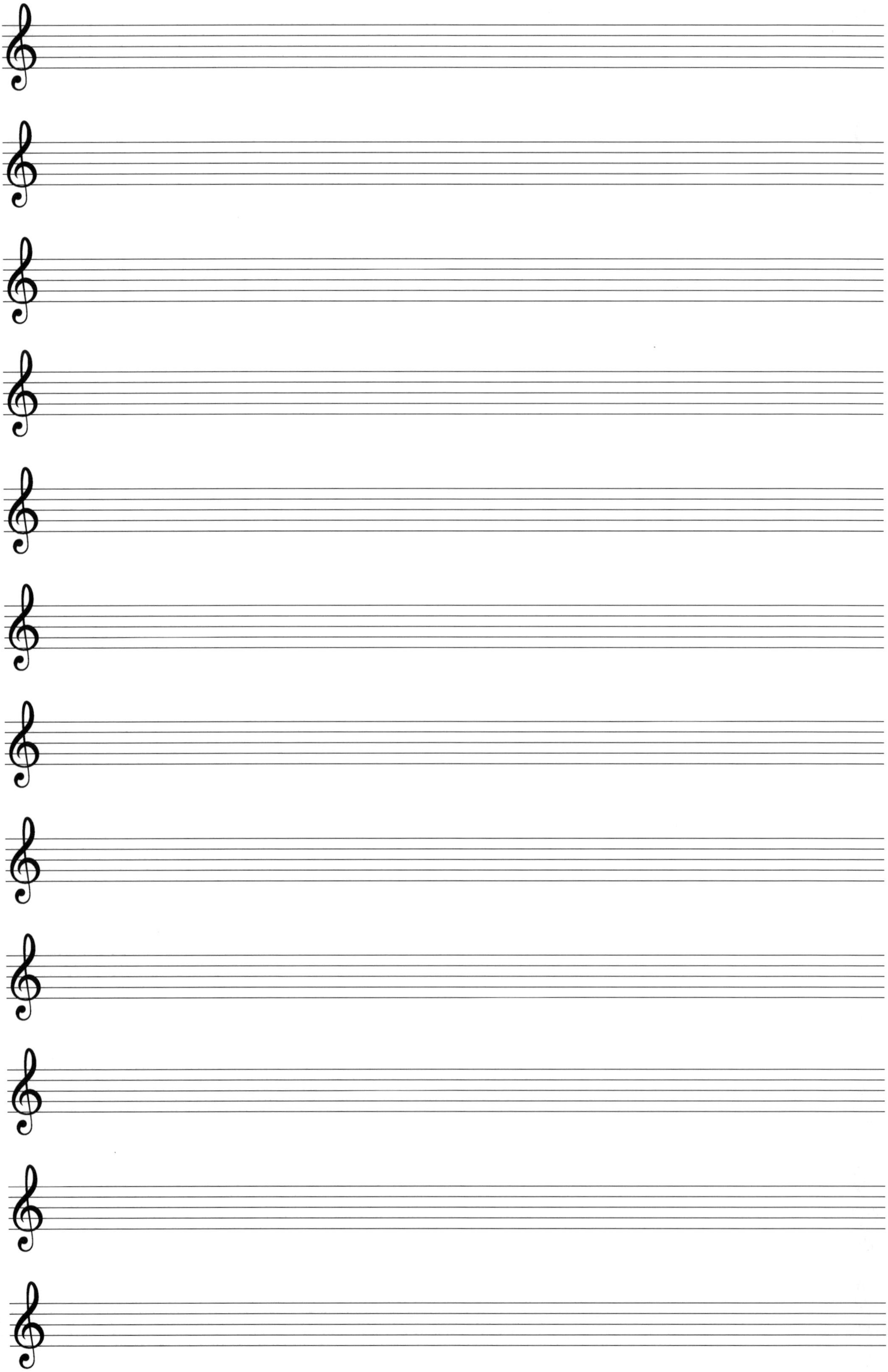

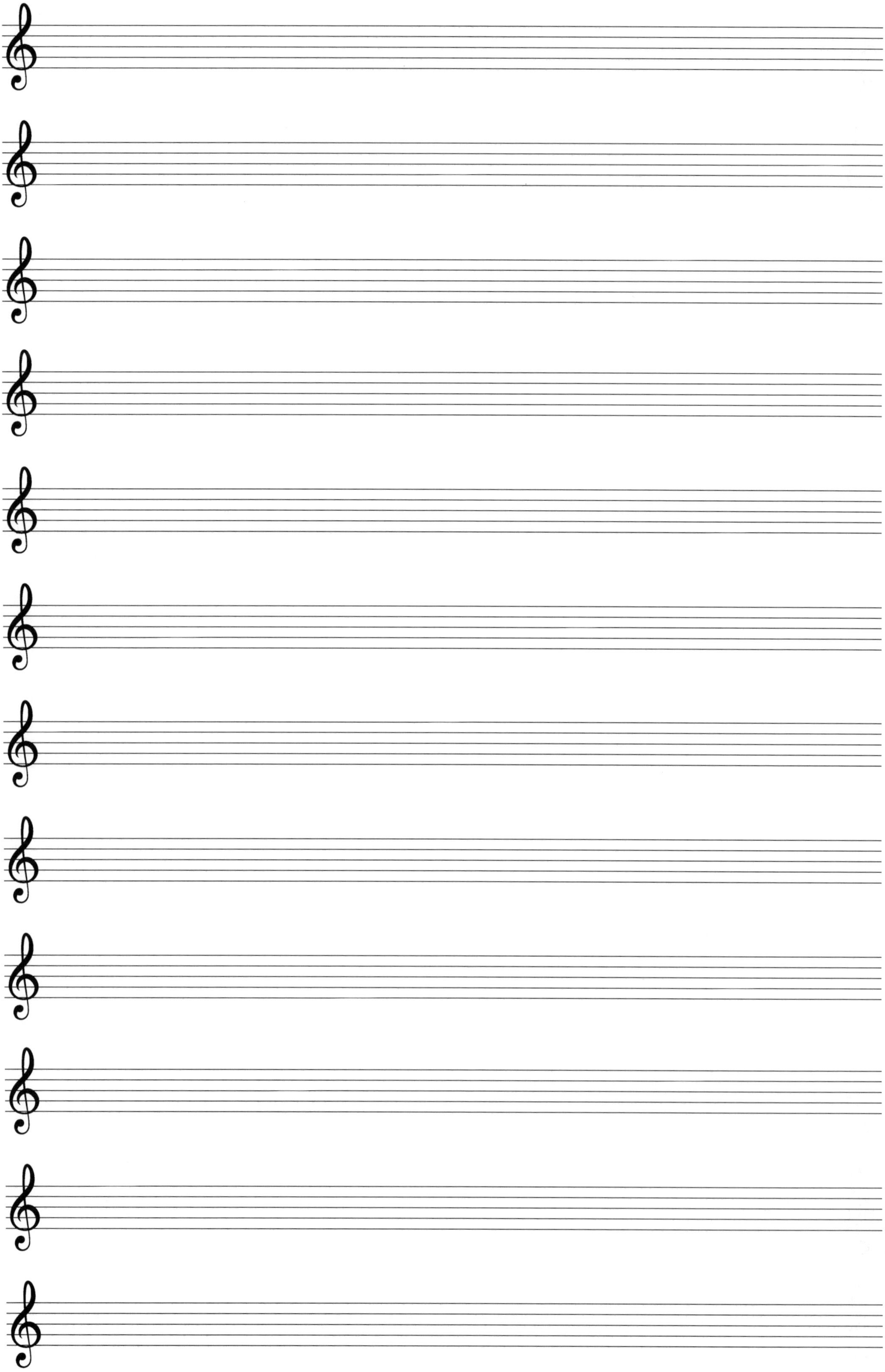

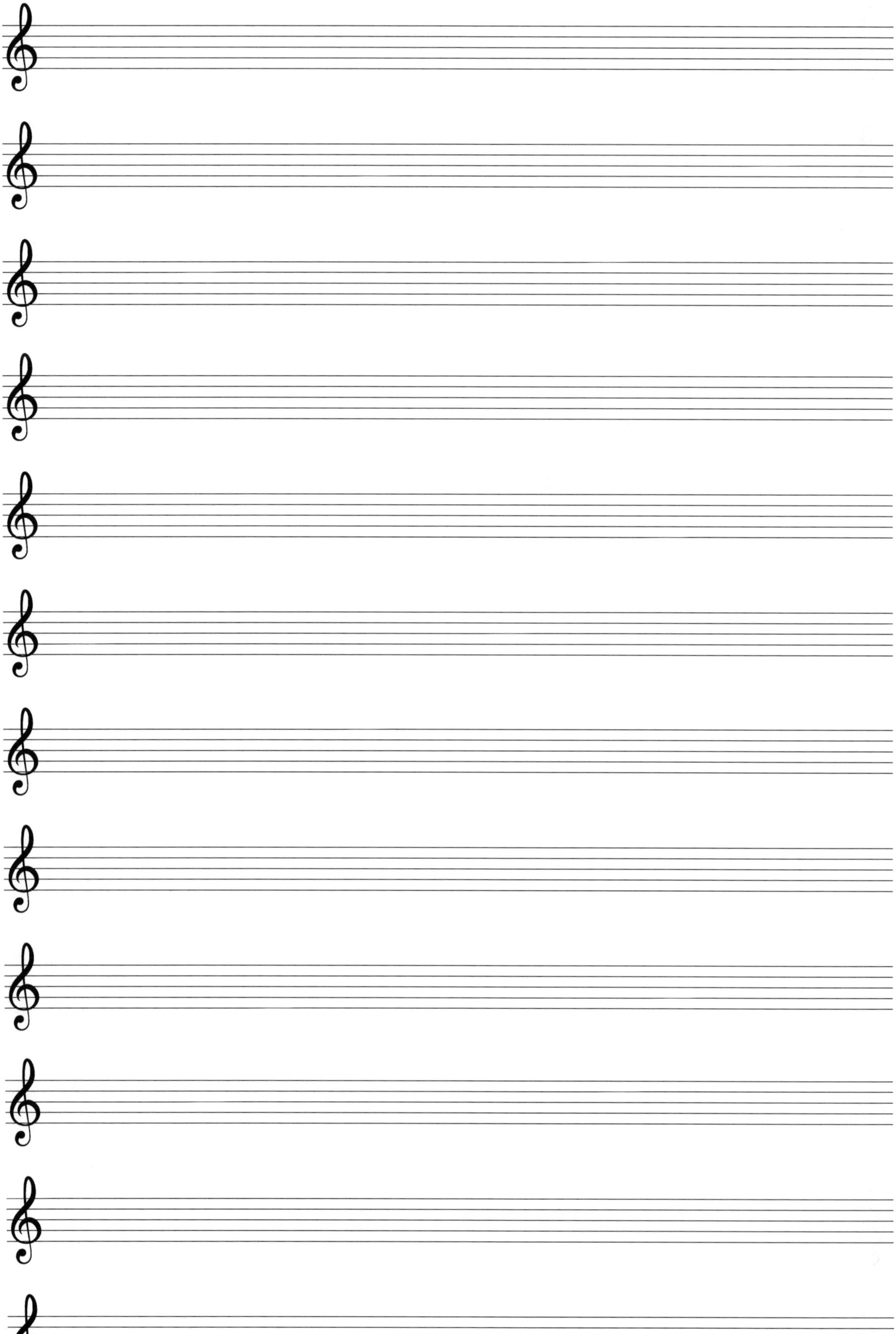

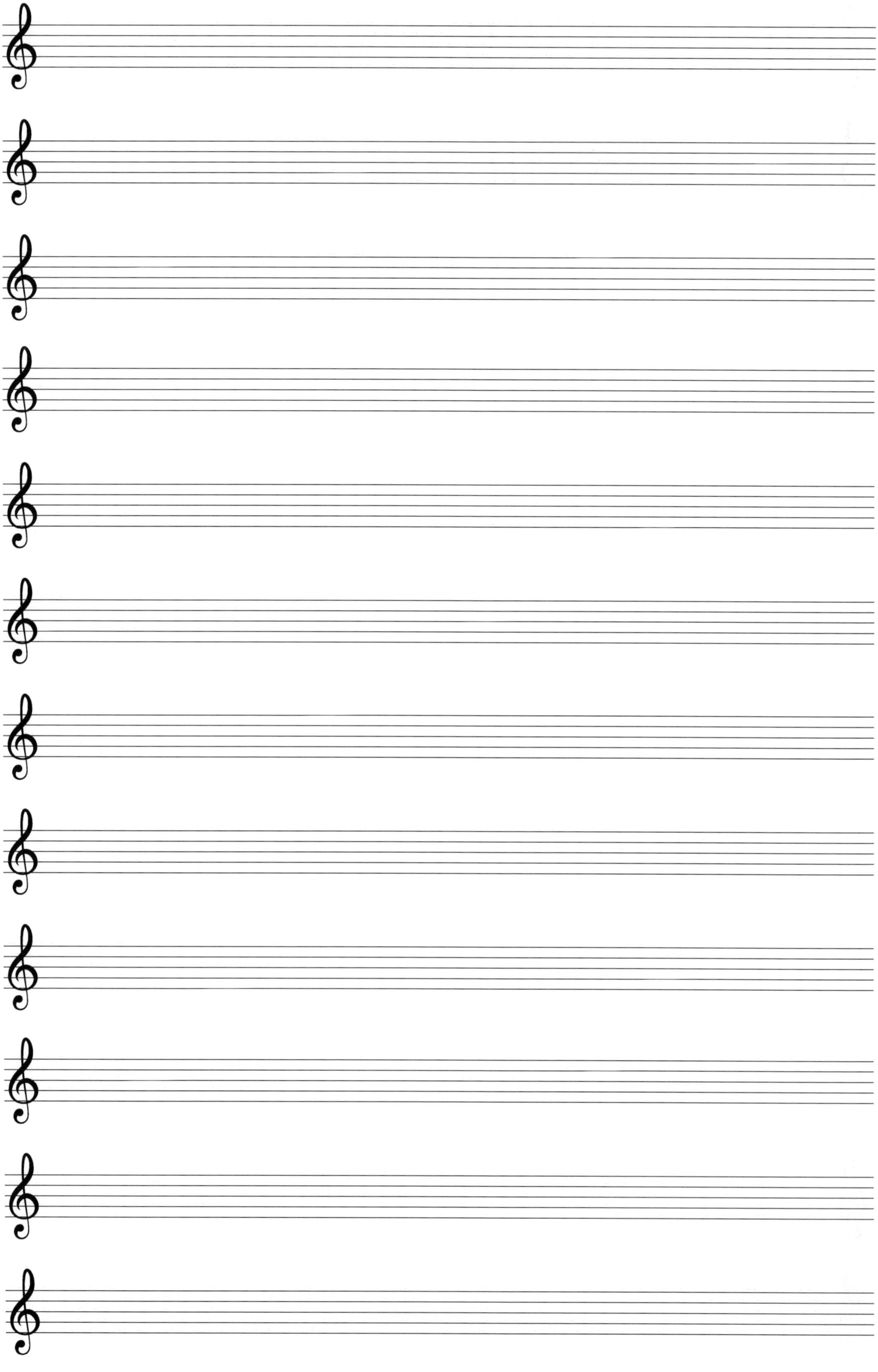

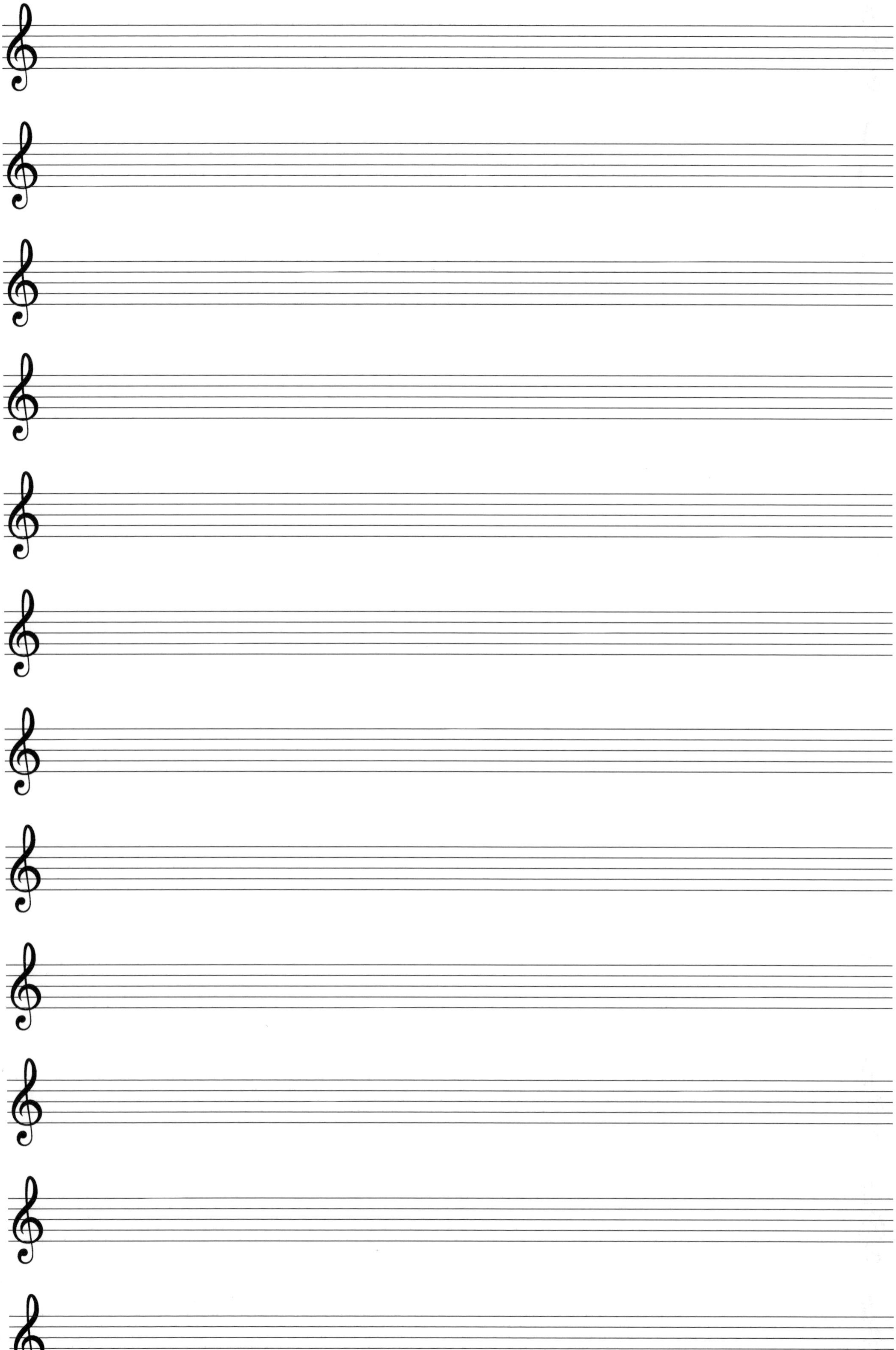

Made in the USA
Monee, IL
03 September 2020

41040631R00065